Also by William Gibson

THE COBWEB

THIS IS A BORZOI BOOK PUBLISHED
BY ALFRED A. KNOPF IN NEW YORK

THE

MIRACLE WORKER

THE
MIRACLE WORKER

A PLAY FOR TELEVISION

by William Gibson

❮❮❮❮❮❮❮❮❮❮❮❮❮❮❮❮❮❮❮❮❮❮❮❮❮❮❮❮❮❮❮❮❮❮❮❮

New York · Alfred A. Knopf · 1957

L.C. catalog card number: 57-10305

© WILLIAM GIBSON, 1956, 1957

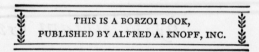

THIS IS A BORZOI BOOK,
PUBLISHED BY ALFRED A. KNOPF, INC.

FIRST EDITION

To the memory of

Anne Sullivan Macy

humbly

Author's Note

This play was produced February 7, 1957, on "Playhouse 90," CBS, with Teresa Wright as *Annie*, Patty McCormack as *Helen*, Burl Ives as *Keller*, Katherine Bard as *Kate*, John Barrymore, Jr., as *James*, and Akim Tamiroff as *Anagnos*. The production was directed by Arthur Penn, who had served as midwife to the script and project from the first word on. Martin Manulis produced.

The present text is meant for reading, and differs from the telecast version in that I have restored some passages that read better than they play and others omitted in performance for simple lack of time.

The main incidents in the play are factual; I have invented almost nothing of Helen's, or of what passes between her and Annie, though often I have brought together incidents separated in time. My chief source has been Annie's own letters of that year, preserved as an appendix to Helen Keller's *The Story of My Life;* these letters, by a girl of twenty-one who seven years earlier could not spell her name, are certainly among the most extraordinary ever written.

For knowledge of Annie's earlier life I am indebted to Nella Braddy's remarkable biography, *Anne Sullivan Macy;* and, for their gracious permission to portray them in these terms, to Miss Keller and her sister, Mildred Tyson; and to Ken McCormick of Doubleday, for his generous help in arrangements.

W. G.

THE

MIRACLE WORKER

ACT ONE

[*It is night, and we are in a child's crib, looking up: what we see are the crib railings and three faces in lamplight, looking down. They have been through a long vigil, it shows in their tired eyes and disarranged clothing. One is a gentlewoman in her twenties with a kindly and forbearing face,* KATE KELLER; *the second is a dry elderly* DOCTOR, *stethoscope at neck, thermometer in fingers; the third is a dignified gentleman in his forties with chin whiskers,* CAPTAIN ARTHUR KELLER. *Their dress is that of 1880, and their voices are southern. The* KELLERS' *faces are drawn and worried, until the* DOCTOR *speaks.*]

DOCTOR

She'll live.

[KATE *closes her eyes.*]

You're lucky, Captain Keller. Tell you now, I thought she wouldn't.

[3]

KELLER [*heavily*]

Doctor. Don't spare us. Will she be all right?

DOCTOR

Has the constitution of a goat. Outlive us all. Especially if I don't get some sleep.

[*He removes his stethoscope, his face leaves the railing; we continue to hear him, but see* KELLER'S *hand across the crib take and squeeze* KATE'S.]

You run an editorial in that paper of yours, Captain Keller, wonders of modern medicine, we may not know what we're curing but we cure it. Well, call it acute congestion of the stomach and brain.

[KELLER *moves after the* DOCTOR, *we hear them off-camera; we see only* KATE'S *tearfully happy face hovering over us, her hand adjusting the blanket.*]

KELLER

I'll see you to your buggy. I won't undertake to thank you, Doctor—

DOCTOR [*simultaneously*]

Main thing is the fever's gone. I've never seen a baby, more vitality, that's the truth. By morning she'll be knocking down your fences again.

KELLER

Anything that you recommend us to do, we'll do—

[4]

DOCTOR

    Might put up stronger fencing. Just let her get well, she knows how to do it better than we do. Don't poke at Providence, rule I've always made it a practice to—

        [But throughout, their voices have been dying out of focus, and the image of KATE'S *face has begun to swim. Music steals in; we hear the music without distortion, but light and sound otherwise are failing.* KATE'S *serene face smiles down with love, blurring in a halo of light, then is a spot, then is gone. Darkness.]*

        [Cut to CAPTAIN KELLER *standing in his yard, inside the gate, lamp in hand, the lighted house behind him; we hear, but do not see the* DOCTOR.]*

DOCTOR

    You're a pair of lucky parents, Captain Keller.

KELLER *[with weight]*

    Thank you.

        [The DOCTOR *clicks a giddy-yap, we hear the clop of hoofs and roll of wheels.* KELLER'S *eyes follow the unseen buggy out of sight, then lift to the stars, thanking them too. Suddenly from the house behind him comes a knifing scream; music out.]*

[5]

[*Cut to* KATE's *face again, not from the baby's eyes, but across the crib, and her look is terrible; she chokes down a second scream.* KELLER *hurries in to her, the lamp aloft.*]

KELLER

Katie!

KATE

Look.

[*She makes a pass with her hand in the crib, at the unseen child's face.*]

KELLER

What, Katie? She's well, she needs only time to—

KATE

She can't see.

[*She takes the lamp from him, moves it before the child's face.*]

She can't *see!*

KELLER [*hoarsely*]

Helen.

KATE

Or hear. When I screamed she didn't blink. Not an eyelash—

[6]

KELLER

    Helen. Helen!

KATE

    She can't hear you.

KELLER

    Helen!

> [*His face has something like fury in it, cry-*
> *ing the child's name;* KATE *almost fainting*
> *takes up the baby's hand, pressing it to her*
> *mouth to stop her own cry. We go close to*
> *her lips, kissing the baby hand. Dissolve on*
> *lips and hand.*]

                ❈❈❈❈

> [*In on a close-up of another pair of lips;*
> *these belong to a Negro girl,* MARTHA, *and*
> *are speaking, but we hear not a syllable. In*
> *absolute silence then a white child's left*
> *hand comes slowly up, to finger over the*
> *lips, which become annoyed in the hand's*
> *direction and scold it.*]

> [*Cut to the lips of a Negro boy,* PERCY,
> *laughing, but also in perfect silence. The*
> *white child's right hand comes up swiftly*
> *to finger over them.* PERCY'S *teeth playfully*
> *bite at it, and the hand jerks away.*]

[7]

[*The silence shatters when we cut to a fuller view,* PERCY's *laughter and other rural sounds at once audible. We are in leaf-dappled sunlight in the yard of the Keller homestead; three children are on the porch steps in a litter of paper-doll cut-outs, and companioned by an old setter,* BELLE. *The white child is* HELEN, *six and a half years old. As we move in on her we see she is in body a vivacious child with a fine head, attractive, but noticeably blind, one eye larger and protruding; her gestures are abrupt, insistent, wild; her face alone lacks lightness, never smiles. Now she has lowered her hands from both faces to her own lips, moving them in imitation, but soundlessly, while we hear* PERCY *laughing, chickens clucking, leaves stirring.*]

PERCY

That's how I do, she keep pokin' her fingers in my mouth, I just bite 'em off.

MARTHA

What she tryin' do now?

PERCY

She tryin' *talk*. She gonna get mad. Looka her tryin' talk.

[*We are close on* HELEN's *face, scowling,*

[8]

*the lips under her fingertips moving in
ghostly silence, growing more and more
frantic, until in a child's rage she bites at her
own fingers. This sends* PERCY *off into more
laughter, but alarms* MARTHA.]

MARTHA

Hey, you stop now.

[*She pulls* HELEN's *hand down.*]

You just sit quiet and—

[*But* HELEN's *hand is again at* MARTHA's *lips,
insatiable, and* MARTHA *slaps it down.*
HELEN's *fingers grope on the step, then
make a scissorslike gesture.*]

PERCY

She want the scissors.

[MARTHA *puts the scissors in* HELEN's *hand,
and instantly* HELEN *has* MARTHA *on her
back, knees pinning her shoulders down, and*
MARTHA's *tied bunchlets of wiry hair are
flying off in snips of the scissors.* PERCY *darts
to the bell string on the porch, yanks it, and
the bell rings.*]

[*Cut to* KATE *opening the door, disturbed.*]

[9]

7

KATE [*for the thousandth time*]
    Helen.

> [*She hurries down the steps to them;* MARTHA *is running off in tears, and* HELEN *is fiercely snipping the shorn bunchlets into smaller fragments.* KATE *reaches to take the scissors,* HELEN *pulls them back, they struggle for them a moment, then* KATE *gives up, wearily, lets* HELEN *keep them. She tries to draw* HELEN *into the house,* HELEN *jerks away.* KATE *next goes down on her knees, takes* HELEN'S *hands, and using the scissors like a doll, makes* HELEN *caress and cradle them, points* HELEN'S *finger housewards.* HELEN'S *whole body now becomes eager; she surrenders the scissors,* KATE *turns her toward the door and gives a little push.* HELEN *scrambles up and into the house, and* KATE *rising follows her back in.*]

> [*Cut into the middle of a conversation in a large old-fashioned room which will serve as living-room and dining-room. Here there is a cradle with a sleeping infant;* CAPTAIN KELLER *in spectacles is working over newspaper pages at a corner desk; a benign* AUNT *with a sewing-basket on a sofa is putting the finishing stitches on a big shapeless doll made out of towels; an indolent young man of*

[10]

> KATE'S *age,* JAMES KELLER, *turns from the window to look at* HELEN. HELEN *halts, her hands alert to grope, and* KATE *turns her to the* AUNT, *who gives her the doll; the* AUNT *meanwhile is speaking to* KELLER.]

AUNT

This Baltimore oculist I hear just does wonders, why, lots of cases of blindness people thought couldn't be cured he's cured.

KELLER [*patiently*]

I've stopped believing in wonders, Aunt Ev.

KATE

But will you write to him, Captain?

KELLER [*patiently*]

No.

JAMES [*lightly*]

Good money after bad. Or bad after good—

AUNT

Well, if it's just a question of money, Arthur—

KELLER

Not money. The child's been to every specialist in Alabama and Tennessee. If I thought it would do good I'd have her to every fool doctor in the country.

[11]

KATE [*simply and relentless*]

> Will you write to him?

KELLER

> Katie. How many times can you let them break your heart?

KATE

> Any number of times.

> [*The foregoing and following dialogue is peripheral to the camera: we are on* HELEN. *She sits on the floor to explore the doll with her fingers, gravely, and her hand pauses over the face: this is no face, a blank area, and it troubles her. Close-up on her fingertips searching for features. She taps questioningly for eyes, but no one notices. She then yanks at her* AUNT's *dress, and taps again vigorously for eyes.*]

AUNT

> What, child?

> [*Obviously not hearing,* HELEN *commences to go around, from person to person, tapping for eyes, but no one attends or understands.*]

KATE [*no break*]

> As long as there's the least chance. For her to see. Or hear, or—

10

KELLER

    I've done as much as I can bear, Katie.

JAMES

    You really ought to put her away, Father.

KATE

    What?

JAMES

    Some asylum. It's the kindest thing.

KELLER [*with force*]

    She's your sister, Jimmie.

JAMES [*retreats*]

    Half-sister, and half mentally defective, it's not pleasant to see her about all the time.

KATE

    Do you dare? Complain of what you *can* see?

AUNT

    What's the child want, Kate?

> [HELEN, *back to her* AUNT, *now yanks two beads off her dress.*]

    Helen!

> [HELEN *pushes the beads into the doll's face.* KATE *comes to kneel, lifts* HELEN'S *hand to*

[13]

her own eyes in question, and HELEN *nods energetically.* KATE *takes pins from the sewing-basket, and pins the beads on as eyes. The* AUNT *inspects her dress.*]

My goodness.

KATE

She doesn't know better, Aunt Ev.

JAMES

Never learn with everyone letting her do anything she takes a mind to. She could have put that child's eyes out with those scissors. Might as well pamper a wild bear-cub in the house here.

KATE [*closing her eyes, wearily*]

I know, I know, what else can I do? If your father won't write to this Baltimore doctor, I will.

AUNT [*indulgently*]

Why, it's worth a couple of beads, Kate, look.

[HELEN *now has the doll with eyes, and cannot contain herself for joy; she rocks the doll, pats it vigorously, kisses it.*]

This child has more sense than all these men Kellers, if there's ever any way to reach that mind of hers.

[*But* HELEN *suddenly is scrambling toward the cradle and unhesitatingly overturns it;*

[14]

the swaddled baby tumbles out, and CAPTAIN KELLER *barely manages to dive and catch it in time.*]

KELLER

Helen!

[*All are in commotion, we hear the baby's screams, but* HELEN, *unperturbed, is laying her doll in its place. Until* KATE *on her knees pulls her hands off the cradle, wringing them in a desperation of anger, tears, impotence;* HELEN *is bewildered.*]

KATE

Helen, Helen, you're not to do such things, how can I make you understand?

JAMES [*easily*]

You've never trained an animal.

KATE

How can I get it into your head, my darling, my poor—

JAMES

You teach them some discipline first thing by—

KATE [*flaring*]

How can you discipline an afflicted child? Is it her fault?

[HELEN's *fingers have fluttered to her mother's distraught lips, vainly trying to comprehend their movements; we are close on these two.*]

JAMES

You didn't hear me say it was her fault—

KATE

Then whose? I don't know what to do! How can I teach her—beat her? When she won't have the faintest notion what it's about or for—

KELLER [*shouldering the infant*]

Katie, it's not fair to Mildred here. We simply can't—

KATE

Are you willing to put her away?

[*Now we see on* HELEN's *face the same darkening rage as at herself earlier, and her hand strikes at* KATE's *lips.* KATE *catches her hand again and* HELEN *begins to kick, struggle, twist.*]

JAMES

Now what?

KATE [*in despair*]

She wants to talk, like—*be* like you and me.

[16]

[*She holds* HELEN *struggling until we hear from the child her first sound so far, an inarticulate weird noise in her throat, such as an animal in a trap would make; and* KATE'S *eyes flood with tears. She releases her, and the second she is free* HELEN *puts herself back in her mother's arms, whimpering to be held;* KATE *embraces, caresses, soothes her.*]

AUNT

I've a mind to take her up to Baltimore myself. If that doctor can't help her, maybe he'll know who can.

KELLER [*presently, heavily*]

I'll write the man, Katie. Today.

[*Dissolve on* HELEN'S *head, hanging down on* KATE'S *arm.*]

❮❮❮❮❮❮❮

[*Close-up of an envelope, stamped and canceled, addressed to "Dr. John Chisholm, 11 Maiden Lane, Baltimore, Md." A hand turns it over, the return address on back is "Capt. Arthur Keller, Tuscumbia, Ala.," and a letter-knife begins to open it.*

Dissolve to CHISHOLM'S *face; he shakes his head.*]

[17]

CHISHOLM

I can't do anything for her. But you might take her to Alexander Graham Bell in Washington—

> [*Dissolve to close-up of an appointment book on a desk, with stamped letters: "Dr. Alexander Graham Bell." A hand opens it and with a quill begins writing an entry opposite a date and hour: "Captain Arthur Keller, with daughter Helen—"*
> *Dissolve to* BELL's *face.*]

BELL

I cannot see any way *in* to her, Captain Keller. I can suggest only that you write to Michael Anagnos at the Perkins Institution in Boston—

> [*Dissolve to close-up of another envelope in* KELLER's *handwriting, stamped, canceled, opened, addressed to "Mr. Michael Anagnos, Director, Perkins Institution for the Blind, South Boston, Mass." This envelope is being lightly slapped in a man's palm, while we begin to hear his voice; when we draw back for a fuller view we find ourselves in a room of the Perkins Institution, listening to* ANAGNOS *as he wanders about, a middle-aged, stocky, bearded man with a Greek accent. The room contains equipment for teaching the blind by touch—a human skeleton, seashells, stuffed animals, models of*

[18]

flowers and plants, embossed books lying open—which ANAGNOS *touches as he walks. The other person in the room is a young woman far in the background, seated beside a desk; we see only her back.*]

ANAGNOS

—child's name is Helen Keller. I then wrote her father saying a governess, Miss Annie Sullivan, has been found. Well. It will be difficult for you there, Annie. But it has been difficult for you here, too. Hm? Gratifying, yes, when you came to us and could not spell your name, to accomplish so much here in a few years, yes. But not easy, always an Irish battle. For independence.

[*We are moving with him around in profile to* ANNIE.]

This is my last time to counsel you, Annie, and you do lack some—by some I mean *all*—what, tact or talent to bend. To others. And what has saved you on more than one occasion here is that there was nowhere to expel you to. Hm?

[*Now we have come full on* ANNIE SULLIVAN, *twenty-one, with a face which in repose is grave and rather obstinate, and when active is impudent, combative, twinkling with all the life that is lacking in* HELEN'S, *and handsome, as long as her eyes are closed; there is a certain crude vitality to her.*]

Your eyes hurt?

ANNIE [*wickedly*]

My ears, ~~Mr. Anagnos~~.

> [*And now she has opened her eyes: they*
> *are inflamed, vague, clouded by the granular*
> *growth of trachoma, and she often keeps*
> *them closed to shut out the pain of light.*]

What's the child like?

ANAGNOS

Like?

ANNIE

Bright or dull?

ANAGNOS

No one knows. And if she is dull, you have no patience with this?

ANNIE

Oh, in grownups, you have to. I mean in children it seems a little—precocious? Can I use that word?

ANAGNOS

Can you spell it?

ANNIE

Well, premature. So I hope she's a bright one.

ANAGNOS

Deaf, blind, mute—no one knows. She is like a little

[20]

safe, locked, that no one can open. Perhaps it is empty. She is given to tantrums.

· Stop

ANNIE

So am I.

ANAGNOS

Yes. Annie, you will find yourself among strangers now, who do not know your history.

ANNIE

Well, that's a kindness.

ANAGNOS

Perhaps you should tell it?

ANNIE [*bristling*]

Why?

ANAGNOS

So they will understand. When you are arrogant.

[*teasing*]

Some must be content with only wealth or family. Not the fortune to be blind, orphaned, in a state poorhouse, until fourteen. Such things go to a young girl's head. Hm?

[*not teasing*]

Annie, be—humble. For your own sake. You will need their affection.

[21]

ANNIE [*dryly*]

And pity, too?

ANAGNOS

Child, we can all use some pity. Not only the afflicted.

[*crisply*]

Well. You are no longer our pupil, we throw you into the world, a working-woman, governess, teacher. *If the child can be taught.* No one expects you to work miracles, even for twenty-five dollars a month. Now, in this envelope, a loan for the railroad, which you will repay me when you have a bank account. In this box, a gift. With our love.

[ANNIE *opens the small box he extends, and sees a garnet ring. She looks up, blinking, and down.*]

Now I think other friends are ready to say goodby.

[*He moves to open the double doors.*]

ANNIE

Mr. Anagnos.

[*Her voice is trembling.*]

Dear Mr. Anagnos, I—

[*But she swallows, and cannot continue un-*

20

til she finds a woebegone joke, in tears and rueful laughter.]

Well, what should I say, I'm an ignorant, opinion-ated girl, and everything I am I owe to you?

ANAGNOS [*smiles*]

That is only half true, Annie.

ANNIE

Which half? I thought I died when Jimmie died, that I'd never again— Well, it's true, you say love, and I haven't *loved* a soul since and I never will, but this place gave me more than my eyes back. Or taught me to spell, which I'll never learn anyway, but it taught me what help is, and how to live again, and I don't want to say good-by. Don't open the door, I'm crying.

ANAGNOS [*gently*]

They will not see.

[*He opens the double doors, and waiting outside is a group of girls, 8-year-olds to 17-year-olds.* ANAGNOS *shepherds them in with a hand; not until they begin to move do we see they are blind.]*

A CHILD

Annie?

ANNIE [*her voice cheerful*]

Here, Beatrice.

[23]

[*As soon as they locate her voice they throng joyfully to her, speaking all at once;* ANNIE *is down on her knees to the smallest, and the following are the more intelligible fragments in the general hubbub.*]

CHILDREN

There's a present. We brought you a going-away present, Annie!

ANNIE

Oh, now you shouldn't have—

SMALLEST CHILD [*mournfully*]

Don't go, Annie, away.

CHILDREN

We did, we did, where's the present? Alice has it. Alice! Where's Alice? Here I am! Where? Here!

[*An arm is aloft out of the group, waving a present;* ANNIE *reaches for it.*]

ANNIE

I have it. I have it, everybody, should I open it?

CHILDREN

Open it! Everyone be quiet! Do, Annie! She's opening it! Sssh!

[*A settling of silence while* ANNIE *unwraps*

> *it. The present is a pair of smoked glasses,*
> *and she stands still.*]

Is it open, Annie?

ANNIE

It's open.

CHILDREN

It's for your eyes, Annie. Put them on, Annie! 'Cause Mrs. Hopkins said your eyes hurt since the operation. And she said you're going where the sun is *fierce*.

SMALLEST CHILD [*mournfully*]

Don't go, Annie, where the sun is fierce.

CHILDREN

Do they fit all right? Did you put them on? Are they pretty, Annie?

ANNIE

I'm putting them on now. Oh, they fit just fine. Why, my eyes feel hundreds of per cent better already, and do you know how I look in them? Magnificent!

CHILDREN [*delighted*]

There's another present! Beatrice! We have a present for Helen, too! Give it to her, Beatrice! Here, Annie!

> [*This present is an elegant doll, with mova-*
> *ble eyelids and a momma sound.*]

[25]

It's for Helen. And we took up a collection to buy it. And Laura dressed it. So don't forget, you be sure to give it to Helen from us, Annie!

ANNIE

It's beautiful. I promise it will be the first thing I give her. If I don't keep it for myself, that is!

SMALLEST CHILD [*mournfully*]

Don't go, Annie, to her.

ANNIE [*her arm around her*]

Sarah, dear. I don't *want* to go.

SMALLEST CHILD

Then why are you going?

ANNIE [*gently*]

Because I'm a big girl now, and big girls have to earn a living. But I'll write, and I'll come back. Some day.

CHILDREN

Will you surely, Annie? Is that a promise, too?

ANNIE

That's a promise.

[*She hugs the smallest child.*]

But if Sarah here doesn't smile for me first, what I'll just have to do is—

[*She pauses, inviting it.*]

SMALLEST CHILD
What?

ANNIE

Put *you* in my suitcase, instead of this doll. And take *you* to Alabama!

[*This strikes the children as very funny, and they begin to laugh and tease the smallest child, who after a moment does smile for* ANNIE. *Dissolve on her smile.*]

[*And in on the earlier contrasting view of* HELEN'S *head, hanging down on* KATE'S *arm.*]

[*Superimpose a close-up of a suitcase tag, which reads, "Anne Sullivan, Perkins Inst. for Blind, Boston, Mass.," and we pull back just enough to see* ANNIE'S *suitcase being carried along by her hand; the suitcase is a bulky thing, halfway between a valise and a trunk. Begin railroad sounds and music. Now we follow two superimposed images, to a background of the railroad noises and music: one is the course of* ANNIE'S *suitcase in close-up, the other is a succession of depot-signs. These read—by daylight, by night light, by daylight again, by*

25

*night light, by daylight—"New York,"
"Philadelphia," "Baltimore," "Washington,"
"Lynchburg," "Roanoke," "Knoxville,"
"Chattanooga."*

ANNIE'S *suitcase travels with her
hand along train aisles, down train steps, up
train steps, rides on valise-racks, sits beside
her skirt at a waiting-room bench. En route
a third image begins to predominate—*
ANNIE'S *face in the smoked glasses, head
back on the seat, sleeping, disturbed by
some dream of terror, until she jerks awake
just on the verge of a scream.*

*She takes off the glasses, and with
a hand-mirror and handkerchief goes after
a cinder in her eye; her eyes are red and
swollen. She peers out the window, and
consults a time-table, her face close to
and moving with the print. She puts the
glasses back on, tries to sleep again, fails; we
see from her mouth how exhausted she is,
miserable, and in pain—something we have
not seen in her face till now, she keeps it out
except when alone. Fade out on her face, in
on the suitcase riding the rack, in on the sub-
sequent depot signs, then her hand hastily
dragging the suitcase down as the sign
"Tuscumbia" comes in, railroad music out,
then freeze on the single image of the sign
"Tuscumbia."]*

[*Pull back to a vestibule view from behind* ANNIE *as she totes her suitcase down the train steps to the depot platform; under the sign* JAMES KELLER *is waiting.*]

JAMES [*coolly*]

Miss Sullivan?

ANNIE [*cheerfully*]

Here! At last, thank heaven.

JAMES

I'm James Keller.

ANNIE

James?

[*The name stops her; we see only her back, but her voice is gentle.*]

I had a brother, Jimmie. Are you Helen's?

JAMES

I'm only half a brother. You're to be her governess?

ANNIE [*lightly*]

Well. Try!

JAMES [*eyeing her, smiles indifferently*]

You look like half a governess.

[ANNIE *is moveless, a blast of steam obliter-*

27

ates them as JAMES *takes her suitcase; the
noise of the engine starts up.*]

[*Cut to* KATE *on a carriage seat, her eyes
eagerly fixed on their approach. As they
near, her face grows doubtful, troubled;
then she makes it pleasant and welcoming,
and* JAMES *is handing a stony-faced* ANNIE
*in her smoked glasses up to the carriage
seat.*]

JAMES

Mrs. Keller, Miss Sullivan.

[KATE *takes her hand, as* JAMES *bears the
suitcase around behind them to load.*]

KATE [*simply*]

We've met every train for two days.

[ANNIE *looks at* KATE's *face and the stone
goes out of her own, the good-humor comes
back to her mouth.*]

ANNIE

I changed trains every time it stopped, the man who
sold me that ticket ought to be tied to the tracks—

JAMES

You have a trunk, Miss Sullivan?

[30]

ANNIE

Yes.

> [*She passes him a claim check, and he dis-
> appears from behind them.* KATE *is studying
> her face, and* ANNIE *returns the gaze, a
> mutual appraisal of a southern gentlewoman
> and a working-class Irish girl.*]

Where's Helen?

KATE

Home.

ANNIE

I can't wait that long.

KATE

Neither can she. There's been such a bustle in the
house, she expects something, Heaven knows what.

> [*Now she voices part of her doubt, not as
> such, but* ANNIE *understands it.*]

You're very young.

ANNIE [*resolutely*]

Oh, you should have seen me when I left Boston.
I got much older on this trip!

KATE

I mean, to teach her.

[31]

ANNIE

> *I* mean to try.

KATE

> Is it possible, even? To teach a deaf-blind child *half* of what an ordinary child learns—has that ever been done?

ANNIE

> Half?

KATE

> A tenth.

ANNIE [*a pause*]

> No.

> > [KATE's *eyes lose their remaining hope, appraising her youth.*]

> Dr. Howe began, but— An ordinary child? No, never. But then I think he made a mistake.

KATE

> Mistake?

ANNIE

> He never treated them like ordinary children.

> > [*She takes the bull by the horns, valiantly.*]

> Don't lose heart, Mrs. Keller, I have three advantages over Dr. Howe that money couldn't buy for you. One

[3 2]

is his work behind me. Another is to *be* young, I've got energy to do anything and nothing else to do! The third is, I've been blind.

[*a pause*]

KATE [*quietly*]

Advantages.

ANNIE

Well, some have the luck of the Irish, some do not.

KATE

What will you teach her first?

ANNIE

Language. I hope.

KATE

Language.

ANNIE

Language is to the mind more than light is to the eye. As Dr. Howe said.

KATE

Language.

[*She smiles, wistfully.*]

We can't get through to teach her to sit still. You *are* young, to have so much—confidence. Do you, inside?

[33]

[ANNIE, *still studying her face, likes it enough to tell the truth.*]

ANNIE

No, I'm as shaky inside as a baby's rattle!

[*They smile at each other, and* KATE *pats her hand.*]

KATE

Don't be.

[JAMES *hoists a small trunk up behind them, comes around, mounts in front of them.*]

We'll do all we can to help, and to make you feel at home. Don't think of us as strangers, Miss Annie.

ANNIE [*cheerily*]

Oh, strangers aren't so strange to me. I've known some all my life!

[KATE *smiles again,* ANNIE *smiles back,* JAMES *shakes the reins, and we dissolve as the carriage commences to move, to a clop of hoofs.*]

❰❰❁❰❁❰❁❰❁❰❁

[*In on a close-up of spectacles being deliberately polished. We draw back enough to see it is* CAPTAIN KELLER, *in his yard, wait-*

> *ing inside the gate. The clop of hoofs draws*
> *nearer,* KELLER *looks up, walks forward.*
> *The moment he clears,* HELEN *is revealed far*
> *behind him: it is a long shot, across the yard*
> *to the porch, and there she stands, a little*
> *motionless figure, her hair tumbled, her pina-*
> *fore soiled, alone on the porch with the*
> *sleeping old setter,* BELLE. *All of the pell-*
> *mell dialogue that follows is off-camera; we*
> *never leave the image of the child on the*
> *porch, solitary and waiting.*]

KELLER

Welcome to Tuscumbia, Miss Sullivan. I take it you are Miss Sullivan—

KATE

My husband, Miss Annie, Captain Keller.

ANNIE

Captain.

KELLER

A pleasure to see you, at last. You had an agreeable journey?

ANNIE

Yes, several! Where's Helen?

JAMES

Where would you like the trunk, Father?

[35]

KELLER

Where you can get at it, I imagine, Miss Sullivan?

ANNIE

If you can, yes—

KELLER

In the hall, I think—

KATE

We've put you in the upstairs corner room, Miss Annie, if there's any breeze at all this summer you'll feel it—

KELLER

And the suitcase—

ANNIE

I'll take the suitcase.

KELLER

I have it.

ANNIE

I want it.

KELLER

No, no—

ANNIE

Let me.

[36]

KELLER

    Not at all, Miss Sulliv—

ANNIE [*impatiently*]

    I've got something in it for Helen. Thank you. When do I see her?

KATE

    There. There is Helen.

    [*Silence now for a moment. Then* ANNIE, *hesitant, enters the yard and our view, lugging her bulky suitcase, and begins the long slow walk, away from us, across the yard to the waiting child.*]

KELLER

    Katie—

KATE

    Ssh.

    [*Nothing else happens, while* ANNIE *walks, stops, walks again. The camera does not move. When* ANNIE *finally reaches the steps she stops again, contemplating* HELEN *for a last moment before entering her world. Then she drops the suitcase on the porch with intentional heaviness,* HELEN *starts with the jar, and comes to grope over it.* ANNIE *puts forth her hand, and touches* HELEN'S. HELEN *at once grasps it.*]

[*Cut instantly to a close-up of their two hands. These hands will be together for the next fifty years, and all of* HELEN'S *knowledge will flow to her through this other hand; something of this should be intimated in this close-up.*]

[*Now* HELEN'S *hand commences to explore* ANNIE'S, *with its garnet ring, like reading a face. Afterward it moves on to* ANNIE'S *forearm, and dress; and* ANNIE *kneels to bring her face within reach of* HELEN'S *fingers and into our view.* HELEN'S *fingers travel over it, quite without timidity, and* ANNIE'S *face is inscrutable until* HELEN'S *hand encounters and removes the smoked glasses; we see* ANNIE'S *eyes grave, unpitying, very attentive.*]

[*Draw back; we are in the doorway.* ANNIE *puts her hands on* HELEN'S *arms, but* HELEN *at once pulls away, and they confront each other with a distance between. Then* HELEN *returns to the suitcase, tries to open it, cannot.* ANNIE *points* HELEN'S *hand overhead.* HELEN *pulls away, tries to open the suitcase again;* ANNIE *points her hand overhead again.* HELEN *points overhead, a question, and* ANNIE, *drawing* HELEN'S *hand to her own face, nods.* HELEN *now begins tugging the suitcase toward the door; when* ANNIE *tries to take it from her, she fights her off and backs through the doorway with it, past us.* ANNIE *stands a moment, then comes into the doorway, her eyes following* HELEN *upstairs, then she climbs past us too.*]

[*Cut to the* KELLERS *watching:* KELLER'S *face is frowning. We leave* JAMES *unloading the trunk, and move with* KELLER *and* KATE *toward the house.*]

KELLER

She's a little rough, Katie. How old is she?

KATE

Twenty-one.

KELLER

A child. What's her family like, shipping her off alone?

KATE

She's very close-mouthed about some things.

KELLER

Why does she wear those glasses? I like to see a person's eyes when I talk to—

KATE

> She was blind.

KELLER [*stops*]

> Blind.

KATE

> She's had nine operations on her eyes. One just before she left.

KELLER

> Blind, good heavens, do they expect one blind child to teach another? Has she experience, at least, how long did she teach there?

KATE

> She was a pupil.

KELLER [*heavily*]

> Katie, Katie. This is her first position?

KATE [*defensively*]

> She's old for her years—

KELLER

> Here's a houseful of grownups can't cope with the child, how can an inexperienced half-blind Yankee school-girl manage her?

> [JAMES *approaches with the trunk.*]

[40]

JAMES [*easily*]

Great improvement. Now we have two of them to look after.

> [*When the trunk clears we move closer to* KATE's *face, troubled, her eyes lifted to the window upstairs.*]

> [*Cut to a close-up of* HELEN's *face in a mirror, wearing* ANNIE's *smoked glasses, her bonnet, and a shawl that swamps her; she cocks her head to one side, then to the other, imitating adult action like a monkey. Draw back to include the room, which is* ANNIE's, *old-fashioned, with brass bedstead and gabled ceiling.* ANNIE *is on the floor beside her open suitcase, watching* HELEN, *amused.* HELEN *comes back to the suitcase, gropes, lifts out a pair of bloomers.*]

ANNIE

Oh, no. No you don't—

> [*But* HELEN, *discarding the bloomers, comes to the elegant doll underneath. Her fingers explore its clothes, its hair, its features, and when she raises it and finds its eyes open and close, she is at first startled, then delighted. She picks it up, taps its head vigorously, taps*]

her own chest, and nods questioningly.
ANNIE *takes her finger, points it to the doll,*
points it to HELEN, *and touching it to her*
own face, also nods.

HELEN *sits back on her heels, clasps*
the doll to herself, and rocks it. ANNIE
studies her, still in bonnet and smoked glasses
like a caricature of herself, and addresses her
humorously, as one might talk to a kitten.]

All right, Miss O'Sullivan. Let's begin with doll.

[*She takes* HELEN's *hand. We go close to the*
hands; in HELEN's *palm* ANNIE's *forefinger*
points, thumb holding her other fingers
clenched.]

D.

[*Her thumb next holds all her fingers*
clenched, touching HELEN's *palm.*]

O.

[*Her thumb and forefinger extend.*]

L.

[*Same contact.*]

L.

[*She puts* HELEN's *hand to the doll.*]

Doll.

JAMES [*off-camera*]

You spell pretty well.

[*Pull back, while* HELEN *sits scowling, puz-*
zled and ANNIE *in one hurried move gets the*

*bloomers swiftly back into the suitcase, the
lid banged shut, and her head turned, to see
JAMES leaning in the doorway.*]

Finding out if she's ticklish? She is.

[ANNIE *regards him stonily, but* HELEN *tugs
at her hand again, imperious.* ANNIE *repeats
the letters, and* HELEN *interrupts her fingers
in the middle, feeling each of them, puzzled.*
ANNIE *touches* HELEN's *hand to the doll, and
begins spelling into it again.*]

What is it, a game?

ANNIE [*curtly*]
An alphabet.

JAMES
Alphabet?

ANNIE
For the deaf.

[HELEN *now repeats the finger movements in
air, exactly, her head cocked to her own
hand, and* ANNIE's *eyes suddenly gleam.*]

How bright she is.

JAMES
You think she knows what she's doing? She imitates
everything, she's a monkey.

[43]

> [ANNIE *now takes the doll from* HELEN, *and reaches for her hand;* HELEN *instantly grabs the doll back.* ANNIE *takes it again, and* HELEN'S *hand, but* HELEN *is incensed now; when* ANNIE *draws her hand to her face to shake her head no, then tries to spell to her,* HELEN *scratches at* ANNIE'S *face.* ANNIE *grasps* HELEN *by both arms, and swings her into a chair, holding her pinned there, kicking, while doll, glasses, bonnet fly in various directions.* JAMES *laughs.*]

She wants her doll back.

ANNIE

When she spells it.

JAMES

Spell, she doesn't know the thing has a name, even.

ANNIE

Of course she doesn't, who expects her to, now? I want her fingers to learn the movements.

JAMES

Won't mean anything to her.

> [ANNIE *gives him a look. She then tries to form* HELEN'S *fingers into the letters, but* HELEN *swings a haymaker instead, which* ANNIE *barely ducks, at once pinning her down again.*]

[44]

Doesn't like that alphabet, Miss Sullivan. You invent it?

ANNIE [*struggling, dodging* HELEN's *kicks*]

Spanish monks under a—vow of silence. Which I wish *you'd* take!

> [JAMES *smiles, bows his head, and leaves.*
> HELEN *is now in a rage, fighting tooth and*
> *nail to get out of the chair.* ANNIE *looks*
> *around desperately. She sees her purse on*
> *the bed, suddenly releases* HELEN, *rummages*
> *in her purse, and comes up with a battered*
> *piece of cake wrapped in newspaper;* HELEN
> *meanwhile has dropped to the floor, is*
> *groping for the doll.*
>
> ANNIE'S *foot moves the doll deftly*
> *out of the way of* HELEN's *groping, and go-*
> *ing on her knee she sets the cake on the back*
> *of* HELEN's *hand.* HELEN *freezes. She sniffs at*
> *it, then her other hand comes across for it,*
> *but* ANNIE *removes the cake and spells*
> *quickly into the reaching hand.*]

Cake.

> [HELEN's *hand waits, baffled.* ANNIE *re-*
> *peats.*]

C, a, k, e. Do what my fingers do, never mind what it means.

> [*She touches the cake briefly to* HELEN's
> *nose, pats her hand, presents her own hand.*

> HELEN *spells the letters rapidly back.* ANNIE *pats her hand enthusiastically, and gives her the cake; and* HELEN *crams it into her mouth with both hands.* ANNIE *watches her, with humor.*]

Maybe I'll steal it back, hm? Now.

> [*She takes the doll, touches it to* HELEN'S *nose, and spells again into her hand.*]

D, o, l, l. Think it over.

> [HELEN *thinks it over, while* ANNIE *presents her own hand. Then* HELEN *spells three letters.* ANNIE *waits a second, then completes the word for* HELEN *in her palm.*]

L.

> [*She hands over the doll, and* HELEN *gets a good grip on its leg.*]

Imitate now, understand later. End of the first les—

> [*She never finishes, because* HELEN *swings the doll with a furious energy, it hits* ANNIE *squarely in the face, and she falls back with a cry of pain, her knuckles up to her mouth.* HELEN *waits, tensed for further combat. When* ANNIE *lowers her knuckles, there is blood on them; she works her lips, gets to her feet, coughs, spits something into her palm, finds the mirror, and bares her teeth at herself. Now she is furious herself.*]

You little devil, no one's taught you *any* manners?
I'll—

> [*But rounding from the mirror she sees the door slam,* HELEN *and the doll are gone, and worse, the key is rattling outside in the lock.* ANNIE *darts over, to pull the knob; nothing gives. She yanks it again.*]

Helen! Helen, let me out of—

> [*The folly of speaking stops her. She rattles the knob, kneels, peers through the keyhole, gets up again. She hurries to the window, looks down, frowns. She comes back, takes a handkerchief, nurses her mouth, stands in the middle of the room, staring at door and window in turn, and so catches sight of herself in the mirror, her cheek scratched, her hair disheveled, her handkerchief bloody, her eyes disgusted with herself. Presently she addresses the mirror, with some irony.*]

Don't worry. They'll find you, you're not lost. Only out of place.

> [*She turns to a pitcher and basin on a stand, puts down what is in her hand, pours some water, dips the handkerchief, and commences to wash her face. We go close to what she has put down: it is a broken tooth. Dissolve.*]

[*In on a water-pump in the yard. We hear voices, off-camera.*]

KELLER

We've looked everywhere, I don't know what she could have done with that key. Steady, now—

ANNIE

I'd really like to—

KELLER

No, no, hold tight. The last occasion she locked her mother in the pantry she was there pounding for three hours. I'll have to have that door taken down—

ANNIE

Captain Keller, I'm perfectly capable of going down a ladder under my own—

KELLER

I doubt it, Miss Sullivan. Simply hold onto my neck.

[*Meanwhile we are slowly drawing back in the yard, where* KATE, JAMES, *a couple of* NEGRO SERVANTS, MARTHA, PERCY, *the setter* BELLE, *are all standing in a wide and somewhat awe-stricken circle, watching* CAPTAIN KELLER *carry* ANNIE *down a ladder from the upstairs window.* KELLER *wobbles, and* ANNIE *grabs at his whiskers.*]

My *neck*, Miss Sullivan.

[*They steady, continue down.*]

—and the lock replaced. The tooth I believe will have to wait until morning, unless you are in such pain that—

ANNIE [*over his shoulder*]

I'm not in any pain, comfortable as can be. I've had worse things—

KELLER

There.

[*He reaches the ground, lets her down.*]

ANNIE

Thank you.

[*She smooths her skirt, looking as unembarrassed as possible.* KELLER *shoos away the spectators.*]

KELLER

Go, go, back to your work. There's nothing here to look at.

[*They break up, move off.*]

Is dinner ready?

KATE

In a few minutes, Captain.

KELLER

Well, let's go in.

> [*They do.* JAMES *is the last to leave, murmuring to* ANNIE *with a gesture.*]

JAMES

Might as well leave the l, a, d, d, e, r, hm?

> [*He goes in too.* ANNIE *stands alone in the yard. Now, we move back around the water-pump, until at its base we see* HELEN *seated, a picture of innocent contentment, playing with the doll. Then her fingers find an opening in its dress, the key suddenly protrudes out of her mouth, and she tucks it away in the doll.* ANNIE *comes around, leans against a fence, and taking off her smoked glasses, studies her.* ANNIE'S *face is impassive for a while, but the twinkle begins to come into her eyes, she shakes her head to herself, and cannot keep a faint smile from appearing on her lips: it is a smile of respect, humor, and acceptance of challenge.*]

> [END OF ACT ONE]

ACT TWO

⟨⟨⟨⟨⟨⟨⟨⟨⟨⟨⟨⟨⟨⟨⟨⟨⟨⟨⟨⟨⟨⟨⟨⟨⟨⟨⟨⟨

> [*Close-up of* ANNIE's *hand writing a letter,
> her smoked glasses lying near by. There is
> also an envelope addressed to* MICHAEL
> ANAGNOS, *and it is his voice we hear off-
> camera, reading the letter.*]

ANAGNOS

". . . and nobody here has attempted to control
her. The greatest problem I have is how to discipline her
without breaking her spirit."

> [*resolute voice*]

"But I shall insist on reasonable obedience from the
start—"

> [*At which point* HELEN's *inky hand comes
> down with a smack, plump on the page.*
> ANNIE's *hand goes into a freeze. Then her
> other hand patiently lifts* HELEN's, *whose
> handprint overlays the page.*]

> [*Draw back, we are in* ANNIE's *room, and*
> ANNIE *is rising from a desk, with* HELEN *in*

57

hand and HELEN *with the doll in hand;* HELEN *as always pulls free.* ANNIE *takes from her bureau a string and two boxes of beads. She presents these to* HELEN's *touch, spells into her hand—*HELEN *is interested in this spelling, though it clearly has no meaning for her—and induces her to sit on the floor.* ANNIE *puts two wooden beads and a glass one on the string, lets* HELEN *feel them;* HELEN *nods and begins to fill the string with wooden beads.* ANNIE *shakes her head no, spells into her hand, takes all the beads off except her initial three, makes* HELEN *feel these again.* HELEN *examines them thoughtfully, tries again, puts on a glass one and two wooden ones.* ANNIE *takes them off, spells into her hand, shows how the wooden ones go on first, the glass one next.* HELEN *comprehends, and proceeds correctly.* ANNIE *gets up, returns to her letter.*]

[*Cut to her hand, writing.* ANAGNOS's *voice resumes.*]

ANAGNOS

"These blots are her handiwork. The more I think, the more certain I am that obedience is the gateway through which knowledge enters the mind of the child—"

[*Cut to* HELEN, *hanging the completed string of beads around her neck, whereupon*

they all slide off the unknotted end. HELEN
*sits darkly. Then with vengeful resolve she
seizes her doll, and is about to dash its brains
out on the floor when* ANNIE, *coming hastily,
intercepts it with her hand.* ANNIE *goes
through the motion of knocking the doll's
head on the floor, spells into* HELEN'S *hand,
lets* HELEN *feel the grieved expression on
her face. Next she makes* HELEN *caress the
doll and kiss the hurt spot and hold it
gently in her arms, then spells into her hand,
lets* HELEN *feel the smile on her face.* HELEN
*sits with a scowl, which suddenly clears;
she pats the doll, kisses it, wreathes her face
in a large artificial smile, and carefully sits
the doll on the washstand. From which she
then takes the pitcher, and dashes it on the
floor instead.*]

[ANNIE *pinches her eyes for patience.*]

◀◈◀◈◀◈◀◈◀◈

[*Dissolve to a close-up of* HELEN'S *hand
fingering a perforated card, with thread on
a needle connecting one row of holes.*
ANNIE'S *hand comes in, demonstrates the
line of thread, then spells into* HELEN'S
hand; HELEN *waits, uncertain.*
Voices speak off-camera.]

KATE

What are you saying to her?

ANNIE

Telling her it's a sewing-card.

KATE

But does she know?

ANNIE

No. She doesn't know what a word is, yet.

KELLER

It's like talking to the fence-post, Miss Sullivan, what possible—

ANNIE

No, it's how you talk to baby Mildred. Gibberish, she can't understand one word, till somehow she begins to.

KELLER

Yes. After how many words, a million?

ANNIE

I guess no mama's ever minded enough to count!

[ANNIE's *fingers meanwhile continue to spell, indicating the card, and* HELEN's *spell back.*]

[54]

KATE

What did she spell?

ANNIE

I spelt card. *She* spelt cake! It's only a finger-game to her now; she's got to learn that things have names, first.

KATE

When will she learn?

ANNIE

Maybe after the millionth word.

KATE [*presently*]

I would like to learn those letters, Miss Annie.

ANNIE

I'll teach you this evening. That makes only half a million each!

[*Her hand meanwhile has shown the needle, and* HELEN'S *hand is threading the card in a haphazard maze from hole to hole.* ANNIE'S *hand tries to instruct hers;* HELEN'S *is impatient, and presently gets rid of* ANNIE'S *simply by jabbing it with the needle; we hear* ANNIE'S *gasp as her hand jerks away.*]

KATE

I'm sorry, Miss Annie. But that's how she is, there are times she simply will not be interfered with.

[55]

[*The next voice we hear is that of a Negro woman,* VINEY.]

VINEY

Breakfast ready!

ANNIE [*a little ominously*]

Yes. I'm the same way myself.

[*Dissolve on* HELEN's *hand threading the card.*]

❰❖❰❖❰❖❰❖❰❖❰❖❰❖❰

[*In on the card again, now crazily completed, beside a full plate. Pull back, we are in the dining-room, where the family is seated at breakfast, with* CAPTAIN KELLER *and* JAMES *arguing the war, and* ANNIE *behind her smoked glasses watching* HELEN. HELEN *has left her chair and is wandering around the table.* VINEY *comes in, sets a pitcher of water on the table;* KATE *lifts the almost empty biscuit-plate with an inquiring look,* VINEY *nods and bears it off, neither of them interrupting the men.* ANNIE *meanwhile sits with fork quiet, watching* HELEN, *who, at her mother's plate, claws her hand into some scrambled eggs, takes what she wants, crams it into her mouth.* KATE *catches* ANNIE's *eyes on her, smiles,*

> *half helpless, half indulgent.* HELEN *moves
> on to her father's plate, and we follow her,
> the male talk a muttering in the background,*
> JAMES's *voice deferential and* KELLER's *over-
> riding.*]

JAMES

—no, but give the devil his due, Father. The fact is we lost the South in May when he outthought us behind Vicksburg.

KELLER

Outthought is a peculiar word for a butcher. All he ever did was—

JAMES

Of course he was a butcher. I say only—

KELLER

And a drunken one, half the war.

JAMES

Agreed. His own people said he was—

KELLER

Well, what is it you find to admire in such a man, Jimmie?

JAMES

Nothing, Father, except that he beat us.

KELLER

He didn't.

JAMES

Is it your contention we won the war, sir?

KELLER

He didn't beat us at Vicksburg. We lost Vicksburg because Pemberton gave Bragg five thousand of his cavalry and that fool Loring marched away from Champion's Hill with enough men to—

JAMES

I think we lost Vicksburg because Grant was one thing no Yankee general ever was before him—

KELLER

Drunk? I doubt it.

JAMES

Obstinate. Simply wouldn't give up, he tried four ways of getting around Vicksburg and on the fifth try he got around. Anyone else—

KELLER

He wouldn't if we'd had a Southerner in command, instead of a halfbreed Yankee traitor like Pemberton—

> [*And so on, as little of it as is needed for
> background talk while the camera is on*
> HELEN, *who is working around ultimately*

[58]

toward ANNIE's *plate. She messes with her hands in* CAPTAIN KELLER's *plate, then in* JAMES's, *gulping down whatever pleases her, both men so taking it for granted they hardly notice. Then* HELEN *comes groping with soiled hands to* ANNIE's *plate, her hand goes to it, and* ANNIE's *hand promptly lifts and removes* HELEN's. HELEN *gropes again,* ANNIE *firmly pins her by the wrist, and removes her hand from the table.* HELEN *thrusts her hands again,* ANNIE *catches them, and* HELEN *begins to flail and make noises; the interruption brings* KELLER's *gaze around.*]

What's the matter?

KATE

You see, Miss Annie, she's accustomed to helping herself from our plates—

ANNIE [*good-humoredly*]

I'm not accustomed to it!

KELLER

No, of course not. No reason you should—

KATE

Perhaps you can give her something, Jimmie, to quiet her—

JAMES

> But her table manners are the best she has. Let's see if this—

> [*He pokes a chunk of bacon at* HELEN'S *hand, which* ANNIE *releases; but* HELEN *knocks the bacon away and stubbornly thrusts at* ANNIE'S *plate,* ANNIE *grips her wrists again, the struggle mounts.* KELLER *rises.*]

KELLER

> Let her, Miss Sullivan, it's the only way we get any peace. I'll get you another plate.

ANNIE [*gripping* HELEN]

> I've got a plate, thank you.

KATE

> Viney! I'm afraid what Captain Keller says is true, she'll just persist in this until she gets her own way. We find—

KELLER [*at the door*]

> Viney, bring Miss Sullivan another plate—

ANNIE [*grimly*]

> I've got my plate, I mean to keep it.

> [*Silence for a moment, except for* HELEN'S

noises as she strains to get loose; the KELLERS
are a bit nonplused.]

JAMES

Ha. You see why they took Vicksburg?

KELLER [*uncertainly*]

Miss Sullivan. One plate or another is hardly a matter to struggle with a deprived child about.

ANNIE

Oh, I'd sooner have a more glorious—

[HELEN *begins to kick,* ANNIE *moves her
ankles to the opposite side of the chair.*]

—issue myself—

KELLER

No, I really must insist you—

[HELEN *bangs her toe on the chair and sinks
to the floor, crying with rage and feigned
injury;* ANNIE *keeps hold of her hands, gazing down, while* KATE, *rising, hurries around
to* HELEN.]

KELLER

She's hurt herself.

ANNIE

No, she hasn't.

[61]

KELLER

I can't bear to hear her cry, will you please let her hands—

KATE

Miss Annie, you don't know the child yet, she keeps—

ANNIE

Well, I know an ordinary tantrum when I see one!

KELLER [*outraged*]

Have you no pity in you, girl?

ANNIE

Pity!

[*She releases* HELEN *to turn equally outraged on* KELLER *across the table; instantly* HELEN *scrambles up and dives at* ANNIE's *plate. This time* ANNIE *intercepts her by pouncing on her wrists like a hawk.*]

For this *tyrant*? The whole house turns on her whims, who's to teach her the sun doesn't rise and set for her? Of course I have no *pity*. You do, though, you do—

KELLER

Katie, for the love of Heaven will you—

KATE [*troubled*]

Miss Annie, please, it will do no good to—

[62]

ANNIE [*no break*]

—because it's easier to feel sorry for her than to help her, isn't it?

KELLER [*stiffly*]

I fail to see where you have helped her yet, Miss Sullivan.

ANNIE

I'll begin this minute, if you'll leave the room, Captain Keller.

KELLER [*astonished*]

Leave the—

ANNIE

Everyone, please.

[*She struggles with* HELEN, *while* KELLER *controls his temper.*]

KELLER

Miss Sullivan, you were sent here as a paid teacher. Nothing more. Not as—

ANNIE

I can't unteach her six years of pity if you can't stand one tantrum! Mrs. Keller, you promised me help.

KATE

I did, yes, but what can I—

[63]

ANNIE

Leave me alone with her.

KELLER

Katie, will you come outside with me? At once, please.

[*He leads,* KATE *and* JAMES *follow him to the door.*]

[*Cut to outside the door,* VINEY *coming to it with biscuits and a plate for* ANNIE; *the group meets her on the threshold and* KEL-LER *impatiently waves her back, they bowl her along.*]

VINEY [*bewildered*]

Heaven sakes.

[*They pass us;* JAMES *turns back in the doorway, with humor.*]

JAMES

If it takes all summer, general.

[ANNIE, *within, releases* HELEN'S *hands, and the child again sinks to the floor, kicking and crying her weird noises;* ANNIE *comes to the door, removing her glasses, pocketing them grimly, and closes the door in our face.*]

70

The key rattles, and JAMES *looks down at the lock. Farther down the hall* KELLER *is wiping his mouth with his napkin, throwing it on a chair, picking a hat from a rack.*]

KELLER

This girl presumes! I'm of half a mind to send her back to Boston before the week is out. And so I will, you can tell her so from me.

KATE

I?

KELLER

Ignorant Yankee snip, what kind of female do they breed up there? I'll teach her to keep her place. I want it clear unless there's an apology and change of manner, she goes back. Will you make that clear?

KATE

Where will you be, Captain, while I—

KELLER

At the office!

[*He slams out the door to the porch.* JAMES *turns to eye* KATE.]

JAMES

Will you make that clear?

[KATE'S *face is a little peeved, and* JAMES *observes it.*]

No. He just lost the war again.

[*He picks a hat from the rack.*]

Don't scuttle the girl, she might deserve a chance.

[*He drifts out the porch door, and* KATE *turns back to contemplate the dining-room door, which stands locked and inscrutable.*]

[*Cut to the dining-room, where* ANNIE *is seated at the table and* HELEN *is still on the floor.* ANNIE *is trying to eat, though each mouthful shows how little appetite she has for it.* HELEN *meanwhile is kicking, making noises, and endeavoring to pull* ANNIE'S *chair out from under her.* ANNIE *waggles to sit more firmly. We go close to* HELEN'S *next attempt to topple the chair, which is unavailing, and her fingers get ready for a pinch at* ANNIE'S *flank.*

We cut to ANNIE'S *face for this shot; she is in the middle of her next mouthful and she almost loses it, her eyes wide with startle; but when she rounds on* HELEN, *the child is coming up with curiosity to feel what* ANNIE *is doing.* ANNIE *lets her follow the movement of her fork to her mouth,*

whereupon HELEN *at once reaches into*
ANNIE'S *plate.* ANNIE *firmly removes her
hand.* HELEN *pinches* ANNIE'S *thigh, a good
mean pinchful.* ANNIE *sits with her mouth
tight.* HELEN *pinches her again, and this
time* ANNIE *slaps her, and* HELEN *is the
startled one now. She pinches* ANNIE *again,
and* ANNIE *slaps her again.* HELEN *gets her
fingers ready for another pinch,* ANNIE *gets
her hand ready for another slap, and after a
moment's deep reflection* HELEN *thinks better of it. Instead she blunders all around the
table to feel who is there, and at empty place
after empty place she looks bewildered. She
touches her cheek, in a gesture which will
be explained later, and waits. Then she
gropes her way to the door, finds it locked,
no key.*

She commences to kick it. ANNIE
*rises, bears her away from it, seats her at the
table, begins to sit.* HELEN *writhes out of her
chair, runs back to the door, tugs and kicks
at it.* ANNIE *rises again, bears her back to the
chair, and* HELEN *escapes back to the door.*
ANNIE *pursues her. Slow dissolve.*]

[*In on the hall view of the door, still locked;
now the Negro child* MARTHA *is at it, peering
through the keyhole. The old setter* BELLE
is with her, HELEN'S *doll hanging from her*

jaw. KATE *comes again with the swaddled* BABY *on her shoulder.*]

KATE

You run along outdoors, Martha.

[MARTHA *backs away, and* KATE *contemplates the door, patting the* BABY *until she burps. Slow dissolve.*]

[*In on the dining-room where this time* HELEN *is sitting forlornly in her chair, next to* ANNIE, *both disheveled. Presently* HELEN *begins to eat her breakfast with her fingers.* ANNIE *puts a spoon in her hand, commences to spell.* HELEN *throws the spoon on the floor.* ANNIE *after a moment rises, lifts* HELEN *bodily out of the chair, forces her hand to pick up the spoon, returns her to the chair.* HELEN *again throws the spoon on the floor.* ANNIE *lifts her out of the chair again, forces her hand to pick it up, returns her to the chair.* HELEN *again throws it on the floor. We dissolve on* ANNIE *lifting her out of the chair once more.*]

[*In on an outside window of the house, where* MARTHA *and the boy* PERCY *are rolling a log up; they mount it, glue their noses*

74

to the window-pane, and VINEY *comes along with a broom.*]

VINEY

Shoo, shoo, never you mind what's goin' on inside there.

[*The children flee,* VINEY *calls after them.*]
You tend your own bizness, you hear me?

[VINEY *mounts the log, and peers in. Slow dissolve.*]

[*In on the dining-room, where this time* HELEN *is seated at the table with* ANNIE *kneeling beside her.* ANNIE *is gripping the spoon in* HELEN'S *hand, compelling her to take up food in the spoon to her mouth.* HELEN *sits with lips shut.* ANNIE *waits a patient moment, then lowers* HELEN'S *hand. She tries again;* HELEN'S *lips remain shut.* ANNIE *waits, lowers* HELEN'S *hand. She tries again;* HELEN *opens her mouth compliantly, accepts the food.* ANNIE *lowers the spoon happily, and* HELEN *spatters the mouthful out at her face.* ANNIE *waits a moment with eyes closed, then takes a tumbler of water and dashes it into* HELEN'S *face, which gasps astonished.* ANNIE *with* HELEN'S *hand patiently takes up another spoonful, brings it to her mouth. Slow dissolve.*]

[69]

75

[*In on the hall view of the door, with* HELEN's *doll abandoned in front of it.* VINEY *comes along, contemplates the door. All is quiet;* VINEY *gives a satisfied smile and bends to pick up the doll, but jumps as there is a new burst of screaming, the knob is rattled furiously, and kicks are rained on the door. They cease as the screaming is borne away.*]

VINEY

Heaven sakes.

[*Suddenly the rattling and kicking begins again, and are as suddenly borne away again.* VINEY *picks up* HELEN's *doll, and it plaintively says momma. Slow dissolve.*]

[*In on* KATE *in a rocker on the porch, mending socks, her face troubled.* MARTHA *runs with a wild leap across the steps, pursued presently by* PERCY, *and* KATE *stops mending to let her gaze follow the children, so envious that her eyes fill with tears.* VINEY *comes out the porch door, a knotted kerchief on her head and a feather-duster in hand.*]

VINEY

What am I gone do, Miss Kate? Almost lunch time, I didn't get to them breakfast dishes yet.

[70]

[KATE *blinks her eyes with a sudden resolve, and sets her mending down.*]

KATE

I can't stand this a minute longer, Viney, I'm going in there.

[*She rises, marches in past* VINEY.]

[*Cut to the hall view of the door; as* KATE *comes, the key rattles and the door is opened.* HELEN *blunders out like a bat out of hell, collides with her mother's knees, and clutches them for dear life.* ANNIE *appears next in the doorway, smoked glasses in hand, and looking as though she had indeed just taken Vicksburg; at her face* KATE *becomes uncertain, glances from* HELEN *to* ANNIE, *and* ANNIE *gives a factual report.*]

ANNIE

She ate from her own plate. She ate with a spoon. And she folded her napkin.

KATE

Folded her napkin!

ANNIE

The room's a wreck, but her napkin is folded. I'll be in my room, Mrs. Keller.

[71]

[*She is passing us in close-up when we hear* VINEY'S *voice, cheery.*]

VINEY

Don't be long, Miss Annie. *Lunch* be ready right away!

[ANNIE *shuts her eyes as at a death sentence, takes a deep breath, and passes on.* KATE *gazes down at* HELEN'S *buried head, with wonder and some pride.*]

KATE

Folded her napkin. Viney, did you hear? Helen folded her napkin!

[*Cut to* ANNIE'S *bedroom.* ANNIE *comes in, closes the door, leans back against it, exhausted. We go close to her face, and it is very young, only a girl's; it should not surprise us when the tears begin to come from under the closed eyelids and down the cheeks. She moves away and lets herself fall across the bed; she lies there sobbing, having herself a good miserable cry. Dissolve.*]

❮❖❮❖❮❖❮❖❮

[*Outside her door, a hand knocking; it is* KATE'S. ANNIE'S *voice is cheerful now.*]

ANNIE

Come in!

> [KATE *opens the door, enters with a trayful of tea things.* ANNIE *is now at her desk, pen in hand, her whole manner back to normal except for an inner excitement.*]

KATE [*lifting the tray*]

To mark your victory. The entire house is agog.

ANNIE

And Helen?

KATE

Very clinging. To me. I reap the benefits.

> [*She sits, hands* ANNIE *a cupful;* ANNIE *takes it to the window and gazes down, deliberating something.*]

She's always been such an un-cuddly child. And of course she's my first, and has my heart, in a way that— You should have seen her before her illness, what eyes she had! Always picking up needles and buttons that no one else could find. And so happy, Miss Annie, such a good-tempered child.

ANNIE [*dryly*]

She's changed.

[73]

KATE

Do you know she began talking when she was only six months? She could say "water." Not really—"wahwah." "Wahwah," but she meant water, she knew what it meant, and only six months—

> [*Her voice is unsteady, she is really trying to placate* ANNIE, *who gazes at her, and suddenly it is out in the open.*]

Miss Annie, put up with it. Please. Like the lost lamb in the parable, I suppose, I love her all the more.

ANNIE

Mrs. Keller, Helen's worst handicap isn't blindness or deafness.

> [*Slowly, not to wound.*]

It's your love.

> [KATE *gazes, while* ANNIE *scowls into her cup.*]

And pity. I'd burn them both out of the dictionary if it was up to me.

> [*She gets away from this, indicates her desk.*]

Writing a letter, to say what I think of things here. It's hopeless.

> [KATE'S *gaze becomes anxious.*]

All of you are so sorry for her you've kept her from becoming a human being.

[74]

KATE

 I don't know what you—

ANNIE

 I think what makes a human being is choosing, Mrs. Keller. Between the easy things and the hard things. You've always given Helen the easy thing, she doesn't know what choice is. She won't come near *me* for days, now. It's useless for me to try to teach her language or anything else here. I might as well—

[KATE *cuts in, fearful.*]

KATE

 Miss Annie, before you came we spoke of putting her in an asylum.

[ANNIE *stares. A pause.*]

ANNIE [*flatly*]

 What kind of asylum?

KATE

 For the mentally handicapped. I visited one. There were *rats*, even in the—

[*She shakes her head.*]

 What else are we to do, if you give up? None of us can help her—

ANNIE [*belligerently*]

 Give up? Who told you I was thinking of giving up? It never entered my head!

[75]

KATE

> You said it was hopeless—

ANNIE

> *Here.* Give up, why, I just now saw what has to be done. To begin!

KATE

> What?

ANNIE

> She has to depend on *me*. For everything. Food, clothing, fresh air—

> [*She twinkles, audacious.*]

—yes, the air she breathes, the one who lets her have it has to be her teacher. Not someone who *loves* her, you have so many feelings they fall over themselves like feet!

KATE

> But how can she—

ANNIE

> It's simple enough, I'll live with her somewhere else.

> [KATE *stares.*]

> Till she learns to depend on and listen to me.

KATE

> For how long?

[76]

ANNIE

As long as it takes.

[*She smiles again at* KATE's *face, shakes her head.*]

I don't want her forever. I thought the garden-house in back would do. Change the furniture, take Helen there after a long ride so she won't recognize it, and you can see her every day. If she doesn't know. Well?

KATE [*slowly*]

I'll have to discuss it with my husband.

[*She ventures a smile, almost mischievous, remembering.*]

Captain Keller had a different proposal. I don't know whether he—

ANNIE [*impatiently*]

Mrs. Keller. I grew *up* in such an asylum. Rats, why, my brother Jimmie and I used to *play* with the rats! You're as innocent as a lamb to me, and Captain Keller too. Maybe he'd like to hear what it will be for Helen to live with street-walkers and people queer in the head, with fits, or D.T.'s, and the babies born with no family, the first year we had eighty, seventy died, and the room we played in was the dead house, where they kept the bodies till they could dig the—

KATE [*stricken*]

Oh, my dear—

[77]

ANNIE

—graves.

[*She is curt with* KATE'S *compassion.*]

No, it made me strong. But Captain Keller wouldn't want to send Helen there.

[*Her eyes twinkle, though* KATE'S *are moist.*]

She's strong enough!

KATE [*a pause, simply*]

Is that who tried to burn it out of you? They didn't.

ANNIE

What?

KATE

Love. Or you wouldn't stay.

ANNIE [*dryly*]

I didn't come here for love.

[*She lifts the tea-cup, as in a toast.*]

I came for money! We'll talk to Captain Keller.

[*She sips. Dissolve.*]

❮◆❮◆❮◆❮◆❮

[*In on* CAPTAIN KELLER *at his littered desk in*

[78]
84

> *the living-room, by lamplight, holding a*
> *cigar, staring. He lights the cigar, blows out*
> *smoke.*]

KELLER

Take her away from us, Miss Sullivan? Do you know what it's like to take care of a child, single-handed, day and night?

> [ANNIE's *voice comes, pleasant.*]

ANNIE

I can use both hands, Captain Keller. You wouldn't prefer an asylum.

> [KELLER *continues to stare. Then* KATE'S
> *voice comes, reasonable.*]

KATE

After all, she did fold her napkin, Captain. It's more than you did.

> [KELLER *blows out smoke, scowls at the*
> *cigar, then turns gloomily back to his desk.*]

KELLER

All right, Katie. I consent to the garden-house. We'll give them two weeks. Be a miracle if she lasts that long.

[79]

KATE

      Two weeks! Miss Annie, can you accomplish anything at all in two weeks?

KELLER

      Anything or not, two weeks, then the child comes back. Two weeks. Yes or no, Miss Sullivan?

      [*Cut to close-up of* ANNIE, *standing against the door, her eyes making fast calculations.*]

ANNIE

      Fourteen days. Maybe it's enough. For only one miracle.

      [*She comes to her decision, hard.*]

      Yes.

              ⅭⅭⅭⅭ

      [*In on the interior of the garden-house. The camera pans around, showing a large room with fireplace, bay-window with seat, and big bed; we stop on the shut door. It swings open; outside,* KATE *has led* HELEN *to it, both in traveling clothes; she gently pushes her into the room.* HELEN *comes in groping, baffled, but interested in the new surroundings.* KATE *is joined on the doorstep by* ANNIE. KATE'S *eyes are fixed on* HELEN, *moist; she finds it hard to leave.* HELEN

[80]

86

*stumbles over a box on the floor and in it
discovers her dolls and other battered toys,
is pleased, sits to them, then becomes puzzled
and wary. She scrambles up and back to her
mother's knees, but* ANNIE *has stepped in,
and it is hers that* HELEN *embraces.* HELEN
*recoils, gropes, touches her cheek in the ges-
ture we have seen before.*]

ANNIE

What's that mean?

KATE

It's her sign for me. Helen, dear.

[*Her voice is choked and her hand is drawn,
involuntarily.*]

ANNIE

No.

[KATE *stops herself. She grasps* ANNIE'S *hand
instead, searches her eyes.* ANNIE *smiles back,
squeezes her hand, and* KATE, *turning, hurries out; as she clears the doorway we see*
CAPTAIN KELLER *waiting on the path.* KATE
*joins him, and together they are gazing at
the doorway,* KELLER *consoling her, when*
ANNIE *closes the door, shutting them out.*
HELEN *starts at the door jar, and now rushes
it.* ANNIE *holds her off.* HELEN *kicks her,*

breaks free, and careens around the room like an imprisoned bird, colliding with furniture, groping wildly, repeatedly touching her cheek in a growing panic. She commences her weird screaming. Cut to ANNIE *against the door, her face concerned, as she murmurs to herself a bit grimly.*]

ANNIE

Two weeks. Well.

[*She takes off her bonnet.*]

❦❦❦❦❦❦

[*Dissolve to a trayful of food. It is in a pair of Negro hands, which set it down on a table.* ANNIE's *hands come, uncover a plate, take it, with a napkin and spoon, to* HELEN, *who is sitting on the floor by the bay-window in a kind of exhausted stupor.*

ANNIE's *hand revives her with the smell of food under her nose;* HELEN *sits up reaching, but* ANNIE's *hands move the plate aside to a stool. Then they put the napkin around* HELEN's *neck and the spoon in her hand;* HELEN *offers no resistance. But when* ANNIE's *hand moves the plate and stool back,* HELEN *drops the spoon and reaches with her hand, and* ANNIE's *deftly removes the plate again.* HELEN *sits darkly, her hand on the*

[82]

86

*empty stool, then gropes, retrieves the
spoon, and sits with it in hand, waiting.*
ANNIE'S *restores the plate, and* HELEN *begins
eating with the spoon, avidly.*]

[*Dissolve to a clock that says eight forty.
The room is in lamplight.* ANNIE *in a voluminous old-fashioned nightgown is tiredly
gathering from the floor a litter of dolls and*
HELEN'S *clothes. She takes the clothes to a
chair and hangs them neatly on it, handling
and patting them into shape with a wry
gentleness. In the bed now we see* HELEN,
also in a little old-fashioned nightgown.
ANNIE *turns out the lamp, lifts the blanket,
slides in beside her, and as soon as her body
touches* HELEN'S *the child bounds out on the
other side.* ANNIE *sits up on an elbow, looks
at her in the moonlight with a what-now
expression.*]

ANNIE

You'll take cold.

[*She gets out again, takes a doll, goes to
where* HELEN *stands, leads her back to bed
with the doll.* HELEN *gets in.* ANNIE *covers
her, walks around, slides in the other side,
and* HELEN *jumps out again.* ANNIE *gazes at
her wearily.*]

[83]
89

Oh, my. Here we go.

[*She gets up again, to lead* HELEN *back, and* HELEN *now fights. This fight in the semi-darkness is different, in that* HELEN *conducts it in a tight-mouthed silence. She kicks, strikes, bites, hangs like a dead-weight, springs like a cat, crawls under the bed, is pulled out, hangs onto chairs and bed-legs, is dumped back in bed, rolls out on* ANNIE'S *side, and begins all over again, but with not one scream out of her, all we hear is her panting and* ANNIE'S *heavy breathing as they struggle in and out of the shadows around the room; and after putting* HELEN *in bed for the third time,* ANNIE *next throws her in with such vigor that the bed collapses.* HELEN *is out at once, waiting for the next coming to grips, and* ANNIE *heaves a worn-out sigh at the bed, then sits on a chair to rest and regard* HELEN, *like a curiosity.*]

What makes you such a pigheaded little jackass? [*pause*] Don't you know I'm a pigheaded *big* jackass? You don't stand a chance. [*pause*] Well.

[*She rises, begins to reassemble the bed.*]

I have all night if you have.

[HELEN *makes a defensive move against nothing.*]

[84]

Don't be impatient. First things first.

[*She heaves the bed together. Slow dissolve.*]

[*In on the lighted windows of the main house, going out one by one. Cut to* JAMES's *face in the night; he is out for a stroll, stops to relight his cigar, and is about to continue when he hears* ANNIE's *voice, crooning a lullaby.* JAMES *listens curiously, then makes his way toward the bay-window of the garden-house. We look in the window with him, the camera panning slowly around. The room in moonlight is a post-battle shambles, chairs overturned, rugs out of place, books knocked to the floor, and so forth, and the clock now says eleven forty; when we come to the bed* HELEN *is in it, curled up tight as near to her own edge as possible, but under a quilt and asleep.* ANNIE *is in a rocker near by, crooning, but not to* HELEN: *it is to Helen's doll, which she is rocking against her breast, patting its diminutive behind, and she herself in her voluminous nightgown looking like a small girl, playing momma.* JAMES *lowers his eyes, a little ashamed of witnessing* ANNIE *with her bristles down. Then he turns from the window and leans back against the outside wall, smoking, listening to the lullaby, with his gaze abstracted and faraway. Perhaps he is remembering another mother. Dissolve.*]

❦❦❦❦❦

[*Cock crow.*]

[*Close-up of* ANNIE'S *hand attempting to spell into* HELEN'S *palm, we see the quilt and* HELEN'S *nightgown sleeve;* HELEN'S *hand pulls away and closes in a fist.* ANNIE'S *tries to open the fingers, and* HELEN'S *hand resists.* ANNIE'S *hand withdraws, and* HELEN'S *little fist sits, closed and obstinate.*]

[*Dissolve to a trayful of food placed by the bay-window, where* CAPTAIN KELLER *appears and taps.* ANNIE, *dressed now, comes to open it. We move to* HELEN, *who, in her nightgown, is sitting on the floor, a picture of stubbornness and despair, surrounded by her scattered clothes.*]

KELLER

On my way to the office, I thought I'd see how you were getting along.

ANNIE

Fine!

KELLER

Where is—

[HELEN *touches her cheek, in her mother sign, waits a moment, sighs.* KELLER'S *voice becomes colder.*]

What's wrong?

ANNIE [*cheerfully*]

Difference of opinion. I thought she should dress herself, she thought she shouldn't.

KELLER

Is this her breakfast?

ANNIE

Yes.

KELLER

She wouldn't eat it?

ANNIE

Oh, she'd love to eat it.

KELLER

But it's almost ten o'clock. Why haven't you given it to her?

ANNIE

She understands I will. When she dresses herself.

[87]

93

She's thinking it over. [*pause*] We've got a lot to think over, in two weeks.

KELLER [*heavily*]

Miss Sullivan.

ANNIE [*cheerfully*]

You gave us two weeks.

> [*We go close to* HELEN's *face, darkly scowling, and down to her fists, still closed and obstinate. But one of them rather sneakily edges over till it encounters her shoe, her fist opens one finger, and the fingertip on the shoe begins to describe a slow, thoughtful circle.*]

>

> [*Dissolve to a close-up of a calendar on a desk. The month is March, Friday the 12th is X-ed out, and* ANNIE's *hand comes with a pencil to X out Saturday the 13th, too.*]

>

> [*Dissolve to a close-up of* ANNIE's *fingers trying again to penetrate* HELEN's *closed fist. In vain.*]

>

> [*Cut to the door, which opens, and* PERCY *enters with a trayful of food. He brings it to*

the table. Panning, we see HELEN, *dressed, sitting very quiet and docile on the floor in a ring of her dolls and toys, taking no interest in any of them.* ANNIE *is on a chair near by, just as quiet, studying her. Then* ANNIE *rises, crosses to the tray to take a piece of cake and a cup of milk, and her voice stops* PERCY *at the door.*]

ANNIE

Want to play a game, Percy?

PERCY [*suspiciously*]

Don't want to play no *doll* game—

ANNIE

Not dolls. A big grown-up game.

[*She leads him by the hand to* HELEN. *They sit on the floor, and* ANNIE *opens* PERCY'S *palm, touches it with her fingers curled open.*]

This is how I play talking to Helen. It's not really talking, of course, she doesn't know what words are yet. But we make letters. This one is c, can you do it?

[*She shows him again, proffers her palm, and he tries it; she corrects his thumb.*]

Show Helen.

[PERCY *touches the back of* HELEN'S *fist.*

HELEN *pulls back automatically, but she sniffs, then her fist opens in recognition and begins to grope for* PERCY.]

In her hand.

[PERCY *makes the letter in* HELEN'S *palm, and* HELEN *at once makes it in his.*]

PERCY [*surprised*]
She do it back!

ANNIE

Oh, Helen knows lots of letters. Here's a. C, a.

[*She makes them in* PERCY'S *hand. He makes them in hers.*]

Try them.

[PERCY *tries the two letters in* HELEN'S *hand, and* HELEN *quickly spells four letters back.*]

PERCY

Huh?

ANNIE

She made c, a, k, e. She doesn't know yet it means this.

[*She breaks a piece, gives it to* HELEN, *who eats it.*]

[90]

PERCY

That's cake!

ANNIE

Isn't it funny she knows how to spell it, and doesn't *know* she knows?

[*She takes* PERCY's *hand again.*]

That's the game, to get her to know she knows. C, a, k, e. K. No, this way. That's right. E. Little finger down. C, a, k, e. Now you can say it back.

[PERCY, *with interest, spells into* HELEN's *hand, but gets the letters mixed up;* HELEN *chokes on the cake with amusement.* PERCY *tries again, falters, and* HELEN *grabs his hand, manipulates his fingers, teaching him. He tries again, succeeds, and* HELEN *pats him on the head. She proffers her hand, he succeeds again, and she pats him on the head so vigorously he winces. She then quickly makes three letters.*]

PERCY

Huh?

ANNIE

She's showing off, she made the letters for cup. Would you like to learn one she doesn't know? Milk.

[*She takes* PERCY's *hand from* HELEN's, *spells into it slowly.*]

97

M, i, l, k. M. No, m is this.

[HELEN'S *hand questions what theirs are up to.* ANNIE *lightly brushes it away, and continues.* HELEN'S *comes back, and tries to get in;* ANNIE *brushes it away again.* HELEN'S *hand now insists, so vehemently that* ANNIE *admits it. She spells into each palm alternately.*]

M. That's right. I, that's easy, just the little finger.

L—

[*They are competing now for her hands to spell back into. We go close to the three hands. Superimpose the calendar again, X-ed out through Tuesday the 16th. Fade out on the calendar, leaving the hands minus* PERCY'S—ANNIE'S *and* HELEN'S, *spelling back and forth, accelerating.*]

❰❁❰❁❰❁❰❁❰

[*Dissolve to a close-up of their hands crocheting.* ANNIE *is teaching* HELEN *the stitch,* HELEN *cannot get it right, and* ANNIE *guides her fingers painstakingly. We hear her voice.*]

ANNIE

In and under. Under. Yes. Good!

[*Her hand pats* HELEN'S *approvingly.*]

Well. At least I'm back to where I can touch you,

[92]

98

hm? Touch and go! Be thankful for small favors, Miss Sullivan, out of little acorns—

> [*Her voice continues without interruption, while we dissolve to a close-up of an egg in* HELEN's *cupped hands.*]

—giant oaks, etcetera. Like an egg. E, g, g. It has a name, the name stands for the thing. Simple, it's as simple as birth. To explain. Helen, Helen, the chick *has* to come out of its shell, sometime.

> [*The shell is cracking, the chick is pecking its way out, and makes it. Cut to* HELEN's *face, astounded, delighted, and pull back to include* ANNIE's, *her eyes on Helen.*]

You come out, too.

> [*She cannot help it, she bends with her mouth to touch* HELEN's *brow, and instantly* HELEN's *face freezes, her head averts.* ANNIE's *face loses its gaiety.*]

> [*Dissolve to the calendar, X-ed out through Friday the 19th;* ANNIE's *voice continues, almost pleading.*]

There's only one way out, for you, and it's language. To learn that your fingers can talk.

> [*Dissolve to close-up of* ANNIE's *hand again spelling into* HELEN's, *the same thing over and over.*]

And say anything. Anything you can think. This is water. Water, Helen.

[*Her other hand comes with a glass, and dips* HELEN's *fingers in. She spells again, her voice weary.*]

Water. It has a *name*.

[*Dissolve to an envelope in a man's hands, addressed to MICHAEL ANAGNOS, and again we hear his voice, reading; meanwhile we dissolve back to the room, where we see* ANNIE *standing, weary and disheartened, staring across the room at* HELEN, *who is seated on a stool, playing with a gossamer scarf over her head.*]

ANAGNOS [*off-camera*]

"—I feel every day more and more inadequate. My mind is undisciplined, full of skips and jumps, and a lot of things huddled together in dark corners. If only there were someone to help me! I need a teacher as much as Helen. I need—"

[*But his voice ends when* ANNIE *breaks into it, crying at* HELEN *across the room.*]

ANNIE

I need help too!

[*She paces, in a kind of anger, around the child's stool.*]

Who, who? How do *I* learn? In all the world there isn't one person who can tell me how to reach you.

> [*She drops to her knees, and takes* HELEN'S *hand.*]

How to tell you that this—[*spells*]—means a *word*, and the word means this *thing*, scarf.

> [*She yanks the scarf from* HELEN'S *face.*]

How do I *reach* you?

> [*Dissolve on* HELEN'S *blind, responseless face.*]

❰❘❰❰❘❰❰❘❰❰❘❰

> [*In on the bay-window, where* KATE *appears with a little cage containing three pigeons. She sets it on the sill, stands quiet, gazing in. Move to* HELEN *on the floor, stringing beads. Then to* ANNIE *at the desk, a dictionary open before her; she is peering closely at the print, slowly copying the word "chrysanthemum" a few times on a page which contains other polysyllabic words similarly repeated. But her eyes are bothering her, she closes them and most gently fingers the eyelids. She is interrupted by* KATE'S *voice.*]

KATE

What are you doing to your eyes?

> [ANNIE *puts her smoked glasses on, and turning, gets up cheerfully.*]

[95]

101

ANNIE

> Learning words.

KATE

> You're not to overwork your eyes, Miss Annie.

ANNIE

> Well, I wouldn't if I didn't have such an under-worked brain! When I spell something to Helen I'd better spell it right.

KATE [*wistfully*]

> How quiet she is. You've taught her that. I wish I could touch her.

ANNIE [*briskly*]

> She's learned two nouns since yesterday. Key, and water.

KATE

> But not that they mean *things*.

ANNIE [*reluctantly*]

> No. It's still a finger-game. Without meaning. But she will.

> [*She comes over, while* KATE *shakes her head in a hopeless way.*]

KATE

> How? *How?*

102

ANNIE [*dryly*]

Let's play our finger-game.

[*She takes* KATE's *hand.*]

She will. And when she does, you'll have a lot to tell each other.

[*She spells something into* KATE's *hand.*]

KATE [*puzzled*]

What?

ANNIE

I said this is the only way women can get writer's cramp talking too much!

[KATE *smiles, rather forlornly, and the two women converse into each other's hand, in silence, practicing.*]

[*Dissolve to the cage of pigeons,* HELEN *feeding them. Her fingers explore the lock.* ANNIE *comes, shows her how to unlock it, lets her feel a pigeon, and spells into her hand.*]

ANNIE

Bird. Bird. It has a *name.*

[*They let the pigeons out, to fly around the room,* HELEN *fluttering her hands in delight.*

ANNIE *follows their flight with a quizzically worried eye, then resigns herself.*]

Oh, well. There's always strong soap and water.

❮❖❮❖❮❖❮❖❮

[*Dissolve to the calendar, X-ed out through Wednesday the 24th.*]

[*Cut to the base of an apple tree in sunlight. We go slowly up the trunk, hearing* ANNIE'S *voice.*]

ANNIE

Tree, tree, tree. It has a *name.*

[*As we mount higher and higher we see shoes, then legs, then* ANNIE *and* HELEN *sitting on a branch with lifted skirts,* ANNIE *spelling into* HELEN'S *hand;* HELEN'S *face is beaming,* ANNIE'S *is troubled.*]

❮❖❮❖❮❖❮❖❮

[*Dissolve to a close-up of one end of a crochet-chain of wool, tied to the bed. We follow this chain minutely, it trails across and down the bed onto the floor, snaking this way and that, past toys, around chairs, across the entire room, apparently endless, and finally disappears into the fireplace in the opposite wall, where we also see* HELEN'S legs. HELEN, *leaving it tied inside, comes out of the fireplace, smudgy but very satisfied, pats herself approvingly on the arm, and lays the wool-chain lovingly against her cheek.*]

[*Cut to a basin of water.* ANNIE *drags* HELEN *to it, and with a face-cloth vigorously scrubs her face. In the middle she stops to spell, grimly.*]

ANNIE

Water. *Water.*

[*Dissolve to a duplicate basin of water.* HELEN *drags her doll to it, and with a face-cloth vigorously scrubs its face. And then pokes her fingers insistently at its palm, in an impish mockery of* ANNIE.]

[*Dissolve to the calendar by lamplight, now X-ed out through Thursday the 25th. Draw back;* ANNIE *is staring at it, pencil in hand, and slowly she makes the final X on the 26th, two solid weeks of X-es.* CAPTAIN KELLER's *voice calls heartily.*]

KELLER

Miss Sullivan! I've brought Helen a playmate.

[ANNIE *gets up tiredly, we turn with her, and see* KELLER *heaving the old setter* BELLE *into the window.* BELLE *jumps to the floor.*]

[99]

I'll send Viney over to help you pack, the crack or dawn tomorrow. Mrs. Keller is so excited at having Helen home, you might think it was a new baby in the house—

> [*Cut to* HELEN *in a chair, wearing* ANNIE'S *smoked glasses and holding the dictionary in her lap, turning its pages, pretending to read. After a moment, while the dialogue continues peripheral to the camera,* HELEN *lifts her head and begins to sniff.* KELLER *is kindly.*]

KELLER

You look very tired. You must be glad, too.

ANNIE

No. I need more time.

KELLER

Miss Sullivan.

ANNIE

Another week.

> [HELEN *scrambles off the chair, to grope about the room; when she encounters* BELLE, *she throws her arms around the dog's neck and squeezes her hard.*]

KELLER

No. See how homesick she is. And we miss her too much. What would another week accomplish?

[100]
106

[*Cut to the adults,* ANNIE *shaking her head.*]

ANNIE

I can't promise anything, but—

KELLER

An agreement is an agreement. You've done so much better than I thought was possible, her manners are so much improved I—

ANNIE [*with desperate impotence*]

She has to learn that everything has its name! That words can be her *eyes*, to everything in the world outside her, what is she without words? With them she can think, have ideas, speak, be reached, there's not a thought or fact in the world that can't be hers. You publish a newspaper, do I have to tell you what *words* are? And she has them already—

KELLER

Miss Sullivan.

ANNIE

—eighteen nouns and three verbs, they're in her fingers now, I need only time to push *one* of them into her *mind*! One, and everything will follow. Give me time alone with her to—

KELLER

Look.

[*He points, and* ANNIE *turns.*

107

> *Cut to* HELEN *playing with* BELLE'
> *claws. She makes letters with her fingers*
> *shows them to* BELLE, *manipulates the dog'*
> *claws.*]

What is she spelling?

ANNIE [*toneless*]

Doll.

KELLER

Teaching a dog to spell. [*pause*] The dog doesn'
know what she means, and she doesn't know what you
mean. If God had meant Helen to have eyes, He woul
have given her them. [*pause*] I'll send Viney to pack in the
morning.

> [*Cut to* ANNIE'S *face at the window,* KELLE
> *leaving.* ANNIE'S *eyes are on* HELEN, *unti*
> *she closes them.*]

ANNIE

I didn't do it. Didn't, and can't.

> [*She leaves the window, sits defeated on the*
> *bed, and regards* HELEN *across the room; he*
> *eyes fill.*]

I don't know how, Helen. Not a soul in the worl
knows how.

108

[*We move from* ANNIE, *in her rock-bottom hopelessness, and go close to* HELEN's *face, concentrated on teaching* BELLE *how to spell. Slow dissolve.*]

[*In on* ANNIE's *sleeping face in moonlight. It is disturbed by some dream of growing terror, the dream we have seen once before on her face, in the train; but this time it lifts her up in a nightmare sweat, her face blind and terrified. She gropes with a hand, touches* HELEN's *body under the blanket, and the scream breaks from her throat.*]

ANNIE

Jimmie!

[*It shocks her awake, she stares at* HELEN's *form, shudders, removes her hand, and as though still in the nightmare hears a faraway voice.*]

JAMES [*off-camera*]

Yes?

[ANNIE *shuts her eyes with a choking moan, covers her ears, stumbles out of bed, and at the basin splashes her face with water. The voice comes again, nearer.*]

109

You called me?

[ANNIE *whirls, and now we see* JAMES *at the bay-window, frowning in.* ANNIE *catches up a shawl, throws it around herself.*]

ANNIE

No, no. What are you doing here?

JAMES

I take a turn around here each night. See that all's well.

[ANNIE *sinks onto the window-seat, her head bent;* JAMES *eyes it.*]

Just a dream?

[ANNIE *nods. After a moment* JAMES *speaks quietly.*]

How old was he?

[ANNIE *darts a glance up.*]

Your brother.

ANNIE [*down again*]

Seven. Helen's age.

JAMES

How did he die?

ANNIE

He couldn't walk any more.

[104]

110

[*She is now talking out the dream, exorcising it, not looking at him.*]

He had a bunch on his hip the size of a tea-cup, a tubercular hip, they said. It kept growing. We lived together in the women's ward, to be near each other, Jimmie had to wear a girl's apron to stay. We were a pair, all right, me blind and him on a crutch in that apron. He kept saying about his hip over and over, It hurts, it hurts. Then he couldn't walk, even with the crutch. I was asleep when it happened, I didn't hear them roll his bed out, but I woke up and felt it wasn't there. So I went into the dead house in the middle of the night and found his bed. And under the sheet I felt his skinny ribs and the bunch on his hip. When I screamed it woke everyone, they dragged me off him. [*pause*] That's the part I dream.

JAMES

How long ago?

ANNIE

Eleven years. This May.

[*She has talked it out now, is calmer.* JAMES *waits.*]

JAMES

And you've had no one to dream about since?

ANNIE [*grimly*]

No. One's enough.

JAMES

> You don't let go of things easily, do you?

ANNIE

> No. That's the original sin.

JAMES

> What?

ANNIE

> Giving up. Jimmie gave up.

> [*A pause, while* JAMES *regards her.*]

JAMES

> You'd be quite a handsome girl if it weren't for your eyes. No one's told you?

> [ANNIE *out of feminine vanity reaches to snatch up her smoked glasses and put them on; she replies tartly.*]

ANNIE

> Everyone. *You'd* be quite a gentleman if it wasn't for your manners!

JAMES [*amused*]

> You wouldn't say that to me if you didn't have your glasses on. [*pause*] Perhaps Helen will teach you.

ANNIE

> What?

[106]

JAMES

That there *is* such a thing as defeat. And no hope.

[ANNIE's *face sets.*]

And giving up. Sooner or later, we do. Then maybe you'll have some pity on—all the Jimmies. And Helen, for being what she is. And even yourself.

[ANNIE *sits for a moment, then without another word gets up and closes the window on him. She turns her back, and* JAMES *leaves.* ANNIE *walks away in the semi-dark room, paces, turns again, and coming to the bed, stands looking down at* HELEN. *Then she goes to her knees, and we move close to their two faces,* HELEN's *asleep and* ANNIE's *grim.*]

ANNIE

No. I won't let you be. No pity, I won't have it. On either of us. If God didn't mean you to have eyes, I do. We're dead a long time. The world is not something to be missed: *I know.* And I won't let you be till I show you it. Till I put it in your hand.

[*She puts her lips to* HELEN's *hand; but* HELEN, *even in her sleep, tugs it free and rolls away.* ANNIE *closes her eyes, on her aloneness.*]

[END OF ACT TWO]

[107]

113

ACT THREE

ⅠⅭ❖ⅠⅭ

[*Daylight close-up of a couple of boxes, packed brimful of* HELEN'S *toys, clothes, linens; they are jogging along in a wheelbarrow.*]

[*Cut to a long view from the water-pump in the Keller yard; the pump is huge in the foreground, and beyond it we see the wheelbarrow approaching, being pushed by a Negro, into the yard, until it looms up and passes us.*]

[*Cut to a close-up of* ANNIE'S *and* HELEN'S *hands;* ANNIE *is spelling, lifting* HELEN'S *hand to her cheek in her mother sign, then spelling again. We are still in the garden-house, and cutting back we see* KATE *wait-*

ing, trembling with such impatience that for the first time she speaks harshly.]

KATE

Let her *come!*

[ANNIE *makes the sign again on* HELEN'S *cheek and gives her a little push. Now* HELEN *understands, and begins groping, trembling herself; and* KATE *rushes to clasp her in her arms, kisses her frantically, and* HELEN *clutches her as tight as she can.* KATE *is inarticulate, crying and repeating* HELEN'S *name again and again, and we move forward past them till we see only* ANNIE *gazing at this reunion, her face grave and impassive.* KATE'S *voice fades as, unseen, she leads* HELEN *out.* ANNIE *then turns to the basin of water, where she takes up an eye-cup, bathes each of her eyes, shakes the eye-cup out, puts it in her purse, puts on her smoked glasses, and turns.*]

[*Cut to a full view of the room, which we now see is stripped bare.* ANNIE *is alone in it, and she is bidding it farewell, gazing around, impassively, a defeated general on the deserted battlefield. Then she walks out the doorway, and closes the door on the empty room. Dissolve.*]

115

((∘((∘((∘((∘((

[*In on a family tableau on the porch of the main house.* HELEN *is sitting on the top step with a couple of presents, unwrapping them,* KATE *in the rocker hovering over her,* BELLE *lying near the baby* MILDRED *in the cradle,* MARTHA *and* PERCY *on lower steps gratefully receiving the wrapping-paper and string as* HELEN *gets rid of it,* VINEY *near by beaming,* JAMES *leaning against a porch post looking on, and even* AUNT EV *is back from Act One.*]

[*Cut to* ANNIE's *bedroom.* ANNIE *is standing at the window, looking down. A knock on her door.*]

ANNIE

Come in.

[*The door opens,* CAPTAIN KELLER *enters.*]

KELLER

Miss Annie. I've been waiting to give you this.

[*He brings her an envelope.*]

Your first month's salary. First of many months, I trust. It doesn't express what we feel. It doesn't even pay for what you've done.

[111]

ANNIE

What have I done?

KELLER

Taken a wild thing, and given us back a child. You've taught her so much that we couldn't.

ANNIE

I taught her two things. Yes, and no. Can do and can't do.

KELLER

It's more than all of us could, in all the years we—

ANNIE

I wanted to teach her what language is.

KELLER

Perhaps you will.

ANNIE

I don't know how. I know without it she's in a dungeon. With it we're all kinfolk, at least we can talk. All I know is to go on, keep doing what I've done, and have— some faith that inside she's— That inside it's waiting. Like water, underground. All I can do is keep on.

KELLER

It's enough. For us.

ANNIE

You can help, Captain Keller.

117

KELLER

How?

ANNIE

Even learning yes and no has been at a cost. Of trouble and pain. Don't undo it. The world isn't an easy place, to let her have her way in everything is a terrible injustice to her!

> [*Her eyes fill, it takes her by surprise, and she laughs at it.*]

And I don't even love her, she's not my child! You've got to stand between that injustice and her. Because *I* will. As long as I'm here.

KELLER

We will. We've learned something too, I hope. [*pause*] Won't you come down, to us?

ANNIE

Of course.

> [*She waves the envelope, cheerfully.*]

I used to wonder how I could earn a living.

KELLER

You do.

ANNIE

Yes, now the question's can I survive it!

118

[KELLER *with a paternal hand on her back guides her to the door. Dissolve.*]

❮❖❮❮❖❮❮❖❮❮❖❮❮

[*Close-up of a water pitcher being carried by a Negro hand; we follow it along the hall, through the doorway, to the dining-room table.*]

[*Pull back, as* VINEY *withdraws her hand; the table is laid for dinner, and the family are taking their places—*HELEN, KATE, JAMES, AUNT EV, *and finally* ANNIE *and* CAPTAIN KELLER. ANNIE'S *chair is, as before, next to* HELEN'S. *There is a babble of voices, nothing important being said, until what* KATE *says quiets everyone.*]

KATE

Will you say the grace, Jimmie?

[*They bow their heads, except for* HELEN, *who reaches to be sure her mother is there.* JAMES *considers a moment, obliges lightly.*]

JAMES

And Jacob was left alone, and wrestled with an angel until the breaking of the day; and the hollow of Jacob's thigh was out of joint, as he wrestled with him; and the angel said, Let me go, for the day breaketh. And Jacob said, I will not let thee go, except thou bless me. Amen.

> [*They lift their heads, and* JAMES *winks across at* ANNIE, *but* AUNT EV *stares.* ANNIE *puts the napkin around* HELEN'S *neck.*]

AUNT

That's a very strange grace.

JAMES

It's from the Good Book, isn't it?

KELLER

Pass the bread, Kate.

AUNT

Well, of course it is. Didn't you know?

JAMES

Yes, I knew.

KATE

Lamb, Miss Annie?

AUNT

Then why ask?

JAMES

I meant it *is* from the Good Book, and therefore a fitting grace.

120

AUNT

Well, I don't know about *that*.

ANNIE

The water, Captain Keller, please.

AUNT

There's an awful *lot* of things in the Good Book
that I wouldn't care to hear just before eating.

> [ANNIE *is filling* HELEN'S *glass from the
> water pitcher when she sees her napkin on
> the floor; she bends, retrieves it, puts it
> around* HELEN'S *neck again, and this time
> sees* HELEN *deliberately yank it off to throw
> it on the floor.* ANNIE'S *face grows quiet,
> as does the talk around the table.*]

JAMES

Well, fitting in the sense that Jacob's thigh was out
of joint, and so is this lamb's.

AUNT

I declare, James—

> [*She stops, and follows everyone's eyes.*
> ANNIE, *with all watching in silence, now
> picks the napkin up, and puts it on* HELEN;
> *and* HELEN *throws it down.* ANNIE *rises, and
> bears* HELEN'S *plate away.* HELEN, *feeling it
> gone, commences to kick the table.* ANNIE,

> *coming back, takes* HELEN'S *hand to lead her away, and* HELEN *grabs her mother's arm.*]

KATE

Miss Annie.

ANNIE

Yes.

KATE [*a pause*]

It's a special occasion.

ANNIE [*hesitates, then*]

No.

> [*She tries to disengage* HELEN'S *hand,* KATE *stops her.*]

KATE

Please.

ANNIE

Captain Keller.

KELLER

We had a little talk, Katie, Miss Annie feels that if we indulge Helen in—

AUNT

But what's the child done?

[117]

ANNIE

She's too old to throw things on the floor.

AUNT

But only a napkin, it's not as if it were breakable!

ANNIE

I'm sorry, Mrs. Keller.

KATE

What is it you want to do?

ANNIE

Take her from the table.

AUNT

Oh, let her stay, my goodness, she's only a child, she doesn't have to wear a napkin if she doesn't want to—

ANNIE [*cutting in*]

You must not interfere.

[*Her voice is level, but it stops* AUNT EV *with her mouth open.*]

KATE

This once, Miss Annie. I've hardly had a chance to welcome her home—

ANNIE

She's testing you.

[118]

JAMES

Or you.

KELLER

How?

ANNIE

She's home, she wants to see what will happen. Mrs. Keller, I know it hurts you, but to teach her everything can't be as she wants is bound to be painful, to everyone. She'll live up to what you ask of her. Keep her to what she's learned, and she'll learn more.

> [KATE *surrenders* HELEN'S *hand. But the moment* ANNIE *takes it again,* HELEN *begins to fight and kick, clutching to the tablecloth and* KATE'S *sleeve.* KELLER *rises.*]

KELLER

All right. I'll keep her to it. Not by sending her from the table.

> [*He comes around, takes* HELEN'S *hands from* ANNIE, *pats them;* HELEN *quiets down.*]

Bring her plate back. I won't see a child of mine deprived of food.

ANNIE

If she was a seeing child, none of you would put up with such—

[119]

KELLER [*crisply*]

She's not. Bring her plate, please.

[ANNIE'S *jaw sets, but she gets the plate, while* KELLER *fastens the napkin around* HELEN'S *neck.* HELEN *permits him.*]

There. It's natural enough, most of us don't like our teachers.

[*He puts a fork in* HELEN'S *hand.* HELEN *sits with it.*]

Very well.

[*He starts back around the table. But* HELEN *is motionless, thinking things over, then with a wicked glee deliberately flings the fork on the floor. After another moment's thought she plunges her hand into her food, crams a fistful into her mouth, plunges her other hand into* ANNIE'S *plate.* ANNIE *moves in, to grasp her wrist, and* HELEN, *flinging out her other hand, encounters the water pitcher; she swings with it at* ANNIE; ANNIE, *falling back, blocks it with an elbow, but the water flies over her and the pitcher tumbles to the floor.* ANNIE *gets her breath, then snatches up the pitcher in one hand, snatches up* HELEN *with the other arm, and commences to carry her out, kicking.* KELLER *is in her way.*]

125

ANNIE

Don't interfere.

KELLER

Where are you going?

ANNIE

Don't undo what I do! I treat her like a seeing child because I *ask* her to see, I *expect* her to see! Don't—

KELLER

Where are you taking her?

ANNIE

To make her fill this pitcher again!

KELLER

We have *servants* to fetch water—

ANNIE

Don't interfere with me in *any* way!

> [*She plows past him with* HELEN *under her arm, out the doorway.* AUNT EV *is astounded.*]

AUNT

You let her speak like that, a girl who *works* for you?

KELLER [*angrily*]

No. I don't.

126

[*He is starting after her when* JAMES *stands up, more resolute than we have seen him.*]

JAMES

Let her go.

KELLER [*rounding*]

What?

JAMES

I said let her go. She's right.

[KELLER *stares.*]

She's right and you're wrong.

[KELLER's *face is unbelieving.*]

[*Cut to an outside view of the house, again with the water-pump huge in the foreground. In the background* ANNIE *comes out of the house, pulling* HELEN *along by her hand, the pitcher in her other hand, down the porch steps and across the yard to us at the pump, until their bodies fill the image.*]

[*Cut to another angle,* ANNIE *is putting* HELEN's *hand on the pump handle, grimly.*]

[122]

127

ANNIE

All right. Pump.

> [HELEN *touches her cheek, waits uncertainly.*]

No, she's not here. Pump!

> [*She forces* HELEN'S *hand to work the handle, then lets go. And* HELEN *obeys. She pumps till the water comes, then* ANNIE *puts the pitcher in her other hand and guides it under the spout, and the water tumbling half into and half around the pitcher douses* HELEN'S *hand.* ANNIE *takes over the handle, to keep water coming, and automatically does what she has done so many times before, spells into* HELEN'S *free palm.*]

Water. W, a, t, e, r. *Water, it has a—*

> [*And now the miracle happens. We have moved around close to* HELEN'S *face, and we see it change, startled, some light coming into it we have never seen there, some struggle in the depths behind it; and her lips tremble, trying to remember something the muscles around them once knew, till at last it finds its way out, painfully, a baby sound buried under the debris of years of dumbness.*]

HELEN

Wah. Wah.

128

[*Cut back.* HELEN *drops the pitcher on the rock under the spout, it shatters. She stands transfixed.* ANNIE *freezes on the pump handle.*]

Wah. Wah.

[HELEN *plunges her hand into the dwindling water, spells into her own palm. Then she gropes frantically,* ANNIE *reaches for her hand, and* HELEN *spells into* ANNIE'S *hand.*]

ANNIE

Yes.

[HELEN *spells into it again.*]

Yes!

[HELEN *grabs at the handle, pumps for more water, plunges her hand again into its spurt and grabs* ANNIE'S *to spell it again.*]

Yes! Oh, my dear—

[*She falls to her knees to clasp* HELEN'S *hand, but* HELEN *pulls it free, stands almost bewildered, then drops to the ground, pats it swiftly, holds up her palm, imperious.* ANNIE *spells into it.*]

Ground.

[HELEN *spells it back.*]

Yes!

[HELEN *whirls to the pump, pats it, holds up her palm, and* ANNIE *spells into it.*]

Pump.

[HELEN *spells it back.*]

Yes! Yes!

[*Now* HELEN *is in such an excitement she is possessed, wild, trembling, cannot be still, turns, runs, encounters a trellis, shakes it, thrusts out her palm.* ANNIE *is at it instantly to spell.*]

Trellis.

[HELEN *has no time to spell back now, she whirls groping, to touch anything, falls on the porch step, slaps it, reaches out her palm, and* ANNIE *while spelling to her cries wildly at the house.*]

Mrs. Keller! *Mrs. Keller!*

[HELEN *scrambles onto the porch, groping, and finds the bell string, tugs it; the bell rings, all the bells in the town seem to break into speech while she reaches out and* ANNIE *spells feverishly into her hand. The door opens,* KATE *and* CAPTAIN KELLER *hurry out;* HELEN, *still ringing the bell, with her other hand touches her mother's skirt, and* ANNIE *spells into her hand.*]

Mother.

> [KELLER *now grabs* HELEN's *hand, and* ANNIE *again spells.*]

Papa. She *knows!*

> [KATE *and* KELLER *go to their knees, stammering, clutching* HELEN *to them, and* ANNIE *steps back to watch the threesome,* HELEN *spelling wildly into* KATE's *hand, then into* KELLER's *hand,* KATE *spelling back into* HELEN's. *Then* HELEN *gropes, feels nothing, turns all around, pulls free, and comes with both hands groping, to find* ANNIE. *She encounters* ANNIE's *thighs,* ANNIE *kneels to her,* HELEN's *hand pats* ANNIE's *cheek impatiently, points a finger, and waits; and* ANNIE *spells into it.*]

Teacher.

> [HELEN *spells it back, slowly;* ANNIE *nods.*]

Teacher.

> [*She holds* HELEN's *hand to her cheek. But* HELEN *withdraws it, not jerkily, only with reserve, and retreats a step. She stands thinking it over, then turns again and stumbles back to her parents. They take her to them, and* HELEN *now begins to weep, not weirdly, but softly, radiantly, and like an ordinary child. Dissolve.*]

(<>·(<>·(<>·(<>·(<

[*Close-up of* ANNIE's *hand, writing a letter on a pad in less than full light. We hear* ANAGNOS's *voice, reading.*]

ANAGNOS

"—highly excited and learned the name of everything she touched, so that in a few hours she had added *thirty new words* to her vocabulary—"

[*Cut to a full shot across the porch. It is getting dark, and the porch is empty now, except for* ANNIE *in the rocker. She has stopped writing, is simply sitting, alone. After a moment the door opens, and* HELEN *comes out, in her old-fashioned nightgown.* ANNIE *turns her head, watches her.* HELEN *feels her way across the porch, rather shyly, and when she touches* ANNIE's *chair she stops. Neither moves for a moment. Then* HELEN *creeps into* ANNIE's *arms, and lifting her face, kisses* ANNIE *on the cheek.* ANNIE *gathers her in, and they hold each other, cheek to cheek. We move in on them, they are motionless, but when we near their hands we see they are talking to each other,* HELEN *spelling into* ANNIE's, *Teacher, Teacher, and* ANNIE *spelling something back, just what we do not know until we are in close-up on the two hands, and hear* ANNIE's *voice, unsteady, whispering.*]

132

ANNIE

I, love, Helen.

[*Dissolve on the two clasping hands.*]

❧❧❧❧❧

[*Now time is flying, we see it flying: a tree is letting go of its autumn leaves, and the leaves are settling around a pumpkin on its vine; and we see another pumpkin, with a face cut into it and a lighted candle within, and* HELEN's *hand and* ANNIE's *hand exploring it, and speaking to each other in a fast dance of fingers; and at a window snow is falling, and inside the family is decorating a Christmas tree, with* HELEN *hanging her decorations too, and laughing; and next we see a flower-bed outside, in which the tulips are poking up out of the ground, and* HELEN *is planting her doll by the feet, and pantomiming to* ANNIE *how she expects the doll to grow as tall as herself; and we dissolve to a letter in a square script,* HELEN's *hand writing with pencil on paper laid upon a board with sunken ruled lines. We hear* ANAGNOS *reading it.*]

ANAGNOS

"Helen will write little blind girls a letter
Helen and teacher will come to see little blind girls

133

Helen and teacher will go in steam car to Boston
Helen and blind girls will have fun
Blind girls can talk on fingers
Helen will go to school with blind girls
Helen can read and count and spell and write like blind girls
Helen is blind
Helen will put letter in envelope
Good-bye
Helen Keller"

[*And in, finally, on the room we have seen once before, in Act One, in the Perkins Institution for the Blind: we glimpse only enough to identify it—the skeleton, the flower and plant models—then we move to the double doors just as* ANAGNOS *is hurrying to them. He swings them open, and outside waiting are* KATE, HELEN, *and* ANNIE. HELEN *comes in at once, as soon as* ANNIE *guides her with a little push, while* ANAGNOS *takes* ANNIE'S *and* KATE'S *hands, welcoming them.*]

[*Cut to a view from behind them, and we see that what* HELEN *is going toward is the group of girls, waiting for her. Her reaching hands encounter theirs, spell into theirs, and instantly they are all around her, squealing with delight, calling her name, spelling into her hand, until she is lost to our view in the*

134

noisy melee of children. KATE *moves toward them, and* ANNIE *and* ANAGNOS *are left alone in the foreground.*]

ANAGNOS

Annie, you have made, what, a wonder, hm?

ANNIE

Oh, she's a wonder. I didn't make her.

[*They watch the playing children.*]

Yesterday she asked me, "What is a soul?"

ANAGNOS

A small girl, such a large question.

ANNIE

I said no one knew. But that we know it isn't the body, it's invisible, and it's the part of us that thinks, and loves, and hopes.

ANAGNOS

A very good answer.

ANNIE

Do you know what *she* answered? "But if I write what my soul thinks, it will *be* visible, and the words will be its body."

ANAGNOS [*a pause*]

Yes. Together you have made a wonder.

[130]

135

[*They watch.*]

And will you stay with us, here, now? Both?

ANNIE [*a pause, then shakes her head*]

No. The world is too big. And we've hardly begun!

[*We linger on* ANNIE'*s face for a moment, and we will not see a more fulfilled one.*]

[*Draw back; we are on the children, and the camera lifts, slowly, to a high and full view of them in the room, in their dark clothes,* HELEN *in her light dress, all holding hands and moving in a circle around the smallest child, chanting. Fade out.*]

[END OF THE PLAY]

William Gibson was born in the Highbridge section of the Bronx in 1914. He was educated in the New York City public schools, at Townsend Harris Hall, and at City College. For almost as far back as he can remember, he has been occupied with writing. His previously published work includes a verse play, *I Lay in Zion* (1947); a volume of poems, *Winter Crook* (1948); *The Cobweb* (1954); and numerous poems and short stories in such magazines as *The American Scholar, Poetry, The New Yorker, Harper's Bazaar*, and *Partisan Review*. Mr. Gibson's verse has won him annual awards from *Poetry*, and in 1951 he received the ANTA playwriting award. With his wife and two children, Mr. Gibson makes his home in Stockbridge, Massachusetts.

A NOTE ON THE TYPE

This book was set on the Linotype in Janson, a recutting made direct from the type cast from matrices (now in possession of the Stempel foundry, Frankfurt am Main) made by Anton Janson some time between 1660 and 1687.

Of Janson's origin nothing is known. He may have been a relative of Justus Janson, a printer of Danish birth who practiced in Leipzig from 1614 to 1635. Some time between 1657 and 1668 Anton Janson, a punch-cutter and type-founder, bought from the Leipzig printer Johann Erich Hahn the type-foundry which had formerly been a part of the printing house of M. Friedrich Lankisch. Janson's types were first shown in a specimen sheet issued at Leipzig about 1675. Janson's successor, and perhaps his son-in-law, Johann Karl Edling, issued a specimen sheet of Janson types in 1689. His heirs sold the Janson matrices in Holland to Wolfgang Dietrich Erhardt, of Leipzig.

Composed, printed, and bound by H. Wolff, New York. Paper manufactured by P. H. Glatfelter Co., Spring Grove, Pa.